JUEVOS!

containing the sketchbook

SHIRU

& also the

INTERVIEW WITH A REAL-LIFE FAERY

t thilleman

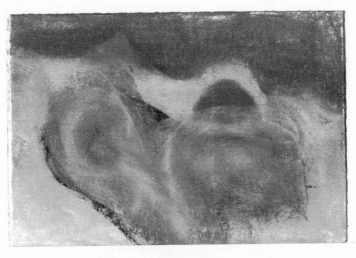

SPUYTEN DUYVIL
New York City

ISBN 978-1-941550-09-0

Library of Congress Cataloging-in-Publication Data

Thilleman, Tod.
 Juevos! : containing the sketchbook Shiru & also the Interview with a
real-llife faery / T. Thilleman.
    pages cm
 ISBN 978-1-941550-09-0
 I. Title.
 PS3570.H453J84 2014
 811'.54--dc23

                        2014020364

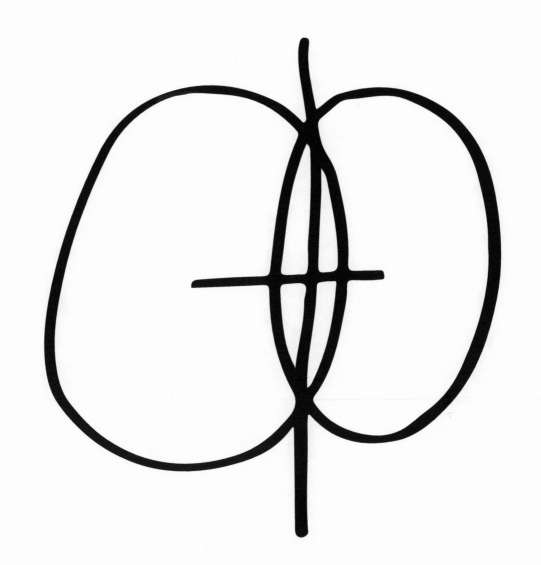

SHIRU

In the museum the largest displays
are his daughters' wedding dresses.
The dress of the daughter who hated him
is ruffles, romantic gossamer.
The dress of the one who honored him
is of classic lines.

Sharon Doubiago, *Hard Country*

The following encounter
took place near the Sea
of Azov during recent
closure of an archeological
zone approximately 300
kilometers east of the towns
of Yeysk and Glafirovsk ....

3/20   After days of Archeo-work
        we heard by our tent   (our own created
                teepee of investigation) sound
                        into patterned
        recognizable design (just as poetry is change
and prose embedded in the *matter* of fiction)
                Scythian artefacts
            at the mound-site
            voice
calling to itself *SHIRU SHIRU SHIRU* … or it
was what I alone began to hear after hastain had
cut his hair   looking every bit the someone I
thought I once knew and so I woke while everyone

was sleeping in camp and jj hastain or his double in the tent too investigated the

voice. It seemed so long since we had left America, where dreams were completely

sent into repetitive overdrive. Every other side had been made unavailable so we

were excited at the prospect of spending a good long time "somewhere else." I

crept back into the tent after observing the motion of stars, some even seemed to

be moving outside their own surrounding blackness, the expansive splayed out

milky way. There were so many stars and they actually appeared to be slithering

into and out of the black. Bright! One star cluster seemed to portray a much more

marked aberration of light. I'm supposed to be recording these observations in

an archeologist's logbook. The asterism flooded my thinking eye (if that is even

possible) so I started writing the different inner appearances of light, previously

contained within my longpoem, but now definitively absorbed into the vast depths

up above. Previously, my name-calling landed the punct on a neo-logism known

as SHIRU, but here it was again as a self-determining voice. I knew, recording the

poem's merges with the mounds at the dig-site, jj was completely right about the merge, how it was all within the shape of those lights as they also merged with the shape of the mounds. Multiple mergers! Their egg-shaped and ovoidal hold on the other fragments and artefacts we were unearthing pointed to one shape and one alone. Something both disturbing and yet exhilarating about that discovery, that realization, and we took the time to recuperate in our tent. Now, as I rested, my chance to catch the merge of all these findings before they spilled out into the vast once again, my grasp in the far forgetful slumber of dreams otherwise to waste as pure fantasy, or psychic projection, back home … what was happening? I felt made over. The voice came thick and hot within me and my throat summoned the edge of the logbook until a ream of notes captured all of it in private ecstasy:

first sketch]

Mind of AHNÁHR must go to PLNIPLOI'S realm

levels all   other realms to defend

one

backing up

disappearance overlaps

(the one   ------>

second sketch]

        eternity figures   he
               sings

        (as the stars spill above of the galactic maw   jj   his off-step-
ping place   another world

third sketch]

        designs itself for infinite encounter
           fleshmatter
          can only dream
             or dreamt connexion
                    sights
               wings

          immense rays

      do you understand the hexeity of this?
        how time is fundamental
          (he
           sings
          AHNÁHR's fat thread

6

fourth sketch]

who
fallen

shape tt now becomes?

fifth sketch}

SHIRU
out of one cloth
become the *poet's* shape

and we were invested in the archaeological
grounded   poet and I   came to form
SHIRU's mouth

upbringing taught his chemical
as well alchemical

out at night with   him
(hem   ?

sixth sketch]

I fell in love his presence recorded by all of us in the
elemental etymologies of temporal materialization   study what he was
love   guise of eternity

accesses mounds
dig-site

seventh sketch]   days and then into nights

hastain moments passing one another
high stones his name joins names in the dig-site mounds
body sleeping next to me   tent we pitch

eighth sketch]

          angels ?   burial chambers ?
                      earth-site ?)

ninth sketch]

                         feeling site
                           gap of site
                             hastain
                         comes to mere sight
                               in the night
                             in dream
                         we own I see and confess

                                  by hem

                         `

tenth sketch]
                         bones | infra-entangling

eleventh sketch]

        sketch of them what they might also be
                    j   and   j   two lie together femur
shin up by the head
    feels bone-growth when looking at the skull?
      missing front teeth   (gap
                    taken all the way
   female
      sharpness   bone's
     taking sight

        site

      sleeps in the tent

twelfth sketch]

     dreaming missing teeth

thirteenth sketch]

I was the earth
wide land became place would allow his
head upon wide open chest

two eyes

piercing animal
black walled human night

m o u n d s!

fourteenth sketch]

Lifetimes gorging on the dark wide gorge
Temporal void opens AHNÁHR
interworld undiscovered

living souls
become flesh   SHIRU's
rites of song
infra-entangled bone-lengths

fifteenth sketch]

Swallowed whole by once-named systems of PLNIPLOI
and   as PLNIPLOI
all's eclipsed

sixteenth sketch]

Dependent upon PLNIPLOI agreement rules (system)
worshipping   play-dating future names
instrumentally silent

we touch in the dark in sleeping ovoidal
tent
pitched black

his back a sickle-shaped bell-curve
I figure from its sight he sees my infra-dreaming
PLNIPLOI's ego capture too

seventeenth sketch]

PLNIPLOI'S signal   (the thought of system)
focus never differentiates nor splits   divides nor
be we to be another
than
its
solitary
(silent
lip design

his

PLNIPLOI
realization
prophecy to fruition   annihilation of atomic leveling
centeredness
his element dirt
inter-pluvial birth of us
when we together be

in

hinting at rain-soaked midst mist
gathers

(hems us here ------>

eighteenth sketch]

yet what image glyphed those mounds   re-moltened by early
foundries   where   study
     ourselves
     hastain con-jectures
         j   to   j?

alchemically bound to *him*
     chemistry PLNIPLOI claims what came first I am writing his true
meaning finally unearthing human history
     opera opus   reasoned by *shi-*
      ru
His *Linga*   stone with no *Sharira*
     (night sky vast here as the first freedom
His   images never an original overlay of movement
     (will show eventually inside burial mounds?
He   cannot understand sketches without us
He   knows indubitably   earth
His   universe broods his body dulls even as it cuts
     (this the twinned realization the present
He   tells other people's story as his own song SHIRU
     (creates their sleep buried images
He   divided ages by families approved
      yet heretofore unheard
     (births out **our**
     gestation finally free for them

of the stone I heard voice speak the tent flaps to worry me into one with them
     (to exit or enter   become *only*   hems

nineteenth sketch]

PLNIPLOI over-hung my thoughts in the former world
And hastain saw as workers see each other working
    so by work man gone from man-kind
        knowing each another now thru work

History eaten whole in the hole of men
  swallowed by thought of him
    tiny tail-blade PLNIPLOI shape over hanging
      space history and sys-   stem
        tongue's syllabus replaces
      any immanent figure

So bodily relevance given to measure
        (gone tent   dreaming
          resting in wide camp's hem surrounds us all

twentieth sketch]

(their early cut word sign or seal

twenty-first sketch]

Scythian's reliquary sounds again the work-site
    ages thru designs the work-site
  imagines evolutionary eschato-skeletons

    AHNÁHR protects SHIRU's singing
        mounting phantom mounds he loves to enter

periphery tail-spin sight I
      otherwise left alone

to collide with colloidal site-spatter   matter
    (stars and planets above us
      sources whose

        re-appearance thru us

TT/ dig logbook   5/1 20__

(beans and kale stain----->)

.... yet what this team was and what of it jj insisted
as we made our way to the site

"If they are all related to the work we do
        then work isn't just a metaphor is it?
    here you see the mound but this could have been the site
        of the Goddess."

My initial response: "This is a team effort. If the determination of the group leads
us down the road toward consensus then that is the thing we have to work with
and I'll stand by that determination as best I can and for as long as I can. But know
it's completely appropriate for me to be confused from time to time and it takes me
a while to pick up the trail. From mounds to Goddess site isn't easy to trace! I'll do
my best."

*Field recording in breast pocket of my parka turned on just here in our
conversation when I inadvertently sat on it. Just found the file and am
running voice recog on it as follows . . . .*

:
:

jj: "You might think a flag would be flown but I can see it won't be that way at all."

tt: "What do you mean?"

jj: "The wood was burnt here … meant to become one with the ground, with the Earth. That's why there's no trace, no matter how or what we sift out of it. She's not going to be found in this kind of winnowing. You have to look at the dirt itself and see what it tells *you*."

tt: "You don't really think this dirt can speak past our symbolic mind into a real discovery do you?! Listen. It's only us. Or to be more specific: it's only me here and I can do anything I want. This dig is practically make-believe as far as I can see. And I see pretty far into it. Into its matter."

jj: "Another way to say it is in an age old and possibly the MOST relevant praxis: trust your instincts!!!!! To do so is a modern feat! It's the boldest and most modern. Just trust your instincts and you'll see what the sight of these wooden poles were meant for. Hold on … have to pee…."

Relative silence, the tent flap sheath unzipped and opened. You can hear me fidgeting inside the tent, looking for my logbook and then wondering if the horses are okay, they snort a bit here on the recording….some distant sound of jj's stream in the latrine aka the weeds and then the horses kind of snorting again I suppose they smell us when we're doing this kind of thing like also when we start to cook they snort and snuffle and shake their heads as if they know something

has changed or as if something is about to change hands, change plac-
es, as if a spirit is behind these shiftings….

jj: (entering the tent in the middle of talking to me, tho I don't
remember this) "…so is really not the aspect of returning to itself.
That is nothing. It's the entering into all change as historical inevi-
tability of her…"

tt: "But I thought we agreed history was not really the entraining
these events would have to be measured by."

jj: "This is a different sense of history. I'm talking about the change
in the history of an organism. That kind of history. Every living
thing lives to enter into its inevitable passing and isn't "mentally"
resistant to that passing and so this is your opportunity to see
the light. There might be images of the resistance recorded in the
layers right next to where these poles were driven into the ground.
That kind of history."

tt: "But what about these symbolic representations carved on the
comb?"

jj: "It's a mirror."

tt: "I meant mirror. I associated the mirror with a comb. Must have
seen it somewhere as a couple."

jj: "Just so! They're inevitably together and can't be pulled apart."

tt: "The evidence suggests this was a burial site. A gathering of
artefacts or hoard, we just have to find out the glint or hint of a
date…"

jj: "That's what I'm talking about: that's what we found. But there's the separate timeline of creations and *that* presents a major impasse. There's a totally separate history at work here. That's exactly why I'm saying this site was a place picked and specifically sited for this mound creation in the same way the other historical timeline came into being. Do you follow me? I'm glad when you can. The essence of the biological was at work. Call it astrological too. But it is a passage along an historical *inevitability*. If we see the inevitable leading to the Goddess then we can see beyond the uses involved here and even beyond the meanings (that's why you have to trust your own intuition). Beyond the meanings of these things and their symbolic associations *we*, you and me, are putting together. We will begin to see ..."

tt: "*I'm* not convinced we won't. I'm just trying to get my mind into ..."

jj: "But it's even on the other side of *that* thought. It's not the self. It's not what you see. It's the vision inherent in ..."

tt: "We haven't unearthed any kind of text tho in order to make that leap."

jj: "It's in seeing the shape of history itself as the inevitable passing on of these shapes ... *is* the prophetic return to their being beyond anything but their initial usage, *their* initial creation. You ..."

tt: "Huh?"

jj: "It's a circle. 360 degrees. The circumference of..."

tt: "We charted the coordinates before: it's the Pleiades here where..."

jj: "Not *that* kind of circle, I mean another kind of recurrence. That's why I'm using the word history here for the first time this way."

A pause in the recorded file. Did I turn it off or did the battery run down? I remember the exchange now. I tried to appear busy and not see what was becoming outlined on jj's face. It was changing in the dark and I was, I admit it, beginning to fall into it. To want to know more. But my initial response had to do with our first meeting and it was slightly choking me, in a good way, and I was wanting to go on making notes, I remember now. I took out my penlight and made some notes in the logbook, even tho it was hard to see what I was writing.

Later, as the night wore on and the silence and darkness seemed to coalesce, I remember falling asleep on top of blankets, fully clothed.

I dreamt. What I recognize of the dream, now that I've acknowledged it, took over my entire horizon. The dream was the completion of my poem to SHIRU. I now know the dream was being conducted by jj. I don't know exactly how that happened, but presence there, in the tent, brought all the minerals in my sleepy being toward the composition of the poem:

Dream mineralization	SHIRU completion
a turkic mantra	set by "Julia" (?) for the pages
SHIRU glimpse	fields
flies	underneath
he sets down now	
it is no longer me	singing
hurls us together	dimensions [sketches]
diamond	known or could be known
bloodies the world	beloved
half-wild	half-servitude
PLNIPLOI	appearance
masks	intimate bond
swaths of immediacy	temporal waxing oceans
SHIRU gathers	Julia's Glossary (who?)
protecting the Tent	horizon of a wide bios
fled on a black horse	discovery
right at the beginning	right at the deserted place

stopped singing	he stands to attention
narrative sequence	Julia dismounts (dream figure?)
wordless	SHIRU later to echo
how *he* follows	the glossary (dream speech?)
empty Tent	Julia (ductus?)
center throne	filled to all employ
hummed Turkic	a burping sound (clef notes)
features elaborate	mono as if to mimic
Julia as PLNIPLOI	material beginnings
Julia	my work (conexxxion?!!!)
pages	sitting
rises from the nostrils	communal
holds	she held me
opening mouth	blows the hems
world away I	tent witness, pegged, pitched
signal moment	storm's approach
	all eyes form horizon

*So, in the dream, at the tent-flap I've gone to look and yet peering out
see a flash of my own precise image staring back in. The flap returned
in a twisting motion torqued such by sudden wild winds. The flap
made finger-like signalings to the center of the tent. There, jj in a stony
trance, still emitting smoke as if from many steppe-inhabitations,
times and cycles of time, generations. The pages of his own notes and
poems now swept up in the dust. I buttoned shut the flaps for the last
time. His pages clung to my dream feet. I read them instantly in my
hand's reaching for them, as the music climaxed in amniotic embrace
of all mineralizations:*

Dear North Star,
     heart-flashes
       Sprung from his face   my hands
           wrystling in depths of you your
  Voice   night's dark also knows
     Oh a-lighting firm melodies
   all yearning   release head-strong and strong cities
  in circles of endless tribute   fire-breathing out for the
last time   Queen or Goddess dear tt
          Your co-mystic, jj

If you were me and set out to reach the stone-faced cast in order to touch, but
then the basalt stone now housing another there, you'd know the sense of flight
possessed my being in our tent, even as it was a dream of my own poem.

Nowhere in this world could that stoned statue be allowed to conduct, from
the center of the world, the interpretation telling me. An obvious allusion to
the sources of possessive vengeance, illogical cunning, heartless totems! All is
emptiness—man—disappearance. I have it in me as that answering appearance or
instigation of the dream itself. All wrapped up.

So, played out the return, this great exhalation of inhabitants, ancient, as well as
modern, and, in mode, I woke.

Wearing my senses and identification of the mounds, measuring them, I made the following notes, hoping to find parameters in our team's work. Later, we could eliminate what was relevant vis-a-vis the list and the levels the markings and their correspondences to the logbook entries   and what was *not* relevant   still to be determined   these mounds have many footed depths to dig into, to disinter the future, and on and on. I felt   in other words   I could set up an ongoing authority for the subjects of each of these objects. They were

Cauldrons which were cast

   (an inscription remaining in part around the base and scribed by cut using some knowledge of early Hittite:

Mirrors

(set into the hats made of felt and other materials fabrics yarns woven into the tall hats the people wore also handled mirrors and the handles had loops or what appear to be loops or hooks of bone with gold and metal work along the clasp of the oval the hand-glass used for gazing or possibly divine work but jj said no when I offered it was a form of current modern self-preening usage no that would require divine-regard self-regard were one and the same the outer form would prevail in other usage whereas glass and mirrors in the hats were not meant for reflection but the opposite of seeing scaring shunning sharply as if their heads were towering out of sight off into the heavens in the one-ness the bringing together the body into the clothes the look of the main man

Somewhere in finding cataloging these things from the mounds   I discovered letters I was using would be interesting if written not so much in a list   but turned into a series of verbs   I was looking for the predicate in all of these things   an effort to write jj and show him the passage from thing to verbal electricity my sensing mounds as a one-ness up to the present

Knives

(sets of sharpening stones also included in the second of the three mounds obvious bronze small blades used for arrows arrow shafts and the larger bronze maybe for digging seemed never to have been sharpened although hilts of leaf swords I picked one up just as I did in the second mound jj let out a gasp as if the contents of the mound shifted deep inside but no sword attached the hilt we breathed a sigh of relief lucky it made us both dive that much quicker with our hands into crevice just created

These notes are being typed on a portable device at
the hotel about 50 km from the site and I'll email them to you
shortly   I've got to head south again   I'll let you know
why later   Yes it's jj-related   hem my own hem is raveling
onto his spool-hem   I'm not using the satellite right now
because I can't   maybe clouds or the Black Sea sending up
too much radiation   I'm using the connection at the hotel
and I know it's risky   nothing I can do about that right
now   I'll just have to let this info cut out of here and into the
world   whomever intercepts it will be anonymously dulled
anyway because they can't see what we've been looking at this
whole entire time out here like the appearance of *three* mounds
for instance

Beavers
      (several workaholic beavers etched and then others from molds onto the
sides of the mounds forges were made became a bit of a question mark we will try
to explain the difference in this land from the previous maybe for a stretch of time
ending not very long ago but preceding for a long time as wetlands the cultural
significance of the beaver its work would have been seen in the making of artefact
as adornment now being uncovered from the mounds even up to the moment
I write in jj's hands we first discover the animals as relationship not so much to
land but something near the term we understand as jj was explaining not just
goddess significance but the hilt of various implements even bowls being part of
land we have no language at present somewhere in the past the embedded sense
of land put not just into parcels of time the sense that time over-all a construction
for pleasure it wasn't completely conceived of yet 3000 years ago in our thinking
so our present belief that land is stationary not portable shows relationship not
only to plunder and rape but other elements of pleasing shape can be taken and
disappeared then reappeared at the drop of a hat what we might call use was
different also sucked into the powerful coursing current of a different time

Menhirs

(the night we were to head north jj left the shared side of the tent I was
sleeping but realized I was alone in the tent or dreaming it and knew I was
involved in some sort of weird relationship maybe even comedic and not serious
but the dreamed aspect of it kept telling me lines to the poems my notebook
open it was a voice coming into the tent from outside the moment light broke
right into me presence and at first I knew it was jj but I was so overcome by
this presence I turned in my sleeping bag as I was naked I felt the color of light
touch every part of me all at once the voices in conversation I was part of that
conversation everything occupied me in sleep making a way into the conversation
as if night itself conversing with day my body staked down in a pleasureful way
as if the white body of me the white body of light's presence were in agreement
and curvaceous in an algorithm of light itself a thread my legs hands staked into
black grass by way of or it was my hair grown longer touching wrists alongside
hips at this I knew it was so much in the affirmative jj had gone where the various
markers in the north were supposed to be situated and too that remaining center
of this conversation between night and day would eventually know the **Men-
hirs** were used for why they had been placed exactly to the north of our site
certainly we had seen the passage of people on a certain night making their way
toward coastal villas vacation retreats along Azov we speculated our team that is
speculated the passage east and west regarding these finds the people must have
left 3000 plus years ago as well the conversation with night day was having in my
half-waking self began to reveal the nature of stones as stelae but also twinned
compassing posts to the other Deer Stones we seemed to take for granted as
herding markers

Deer Stones

(herds of more domestic animals including horses the people tied to *these*
posts also tied within a roaming sense too because the marker used to determine
the ranges of wandering to measure so jj and I walked one stone to another trying
to figure the distance my strides a little dainty yet he could tell them as mine that

way beginning to see as if sight were new to me without a horse or other vehicle and close to the ground I was able to experience my colleague in a different setting out away from the mounds I began to want to visit the mounds and forget about the distance between stones the finds in the mounds beginning to keep me up at night jj seemed never to trouble too much about them because every time I'd look to the other side of the tent REM lightly playing the eyelids but other than that no signs of lingering in a late-night wakeful state like I myself was experiencing but they say man sleeps like 1/3 of his life while the other two-thirds are …. stones had at one time markings that indicated positions the stars too herding at night one would have to follow the flickerings of familiar lights familiar only thru effort of the mnemonic on the post stone were they able to find a place decide to meet gather so that on the stelae all were gathering as if in a dream-summons we began to draw maps of the stones where they had been reported on the steppe and sensed they had to have been driven in deep but this would not have posed a problem because land was much more swampy so many years ago these were very long stelae they had been driven deep their positions always thought to conjure according to constellations in the ancient world as if a reflection the literal sky but it was evident and jj reminded many times mnemonic markings had nothing to do with position of the stelae rather it was the calendrical revelation they contained their positions vis-a-vis the tribe how the Queen or Goddess would have been the center pole in fact I was standing right there at that apex axial spot certainly it would have been cyclical seasonal monthly visits to the stones wrote designs etched them with knowledge of direction via stars the nightsky too but not solely because of them as if in some sort of harem of stars the message of the markings would not have been for any other purpose but to find north south east west via any and all constellations any and all possible visitations so unlike an arrow pointing toward the next stelae designs markings would enable direction to be born out over time while traveling over land while sidereal constellations likewise moving changing over time much like referring to a compass markings told of changes in the nightsky would completely lose track horizontal direction instead focus herders travelers upon relative certainties they'd need to coordinate their *own* journey

Incisions on Shards

        (we don't know what these are hastain seems to think something
from a ritualized incantated initiation ceremony I'm inclined to think a
paramecium thrived when the area was more flooded wet so they might be designs
or simply trails each and every one another microbial universe a kind of larvae
in legions left on bones or petrified stumps of trees perhaps legends of meals
eaten perhaps consumed and transformed into energy in a biological epoch now
completely vanished and if jj is right then the people here were certainly complex
enough to have multi-dimensional visionary experiences the designs so random
seeming and yet natural they could have been carved by trance that I'll grant you
every time without exception as I'm totally open to the above possibility always
and forever now especially now that I can hear myself speaking on and on about
them

Wondering the significance of what I sent to the main office. Am cutting and pasting the printout here in the hotel room in Yeysk :

Attached please find our local readings for
soil analysis inside the mounds.

scythsoilanaly.docx

Date: Wed, 14 July 20__ 03:32:48 -0400
From: tt@amerarch.org
To: h23hmarcheologos@amerarch.org
Subject: re: re: re: re: local sampling data

Included in the soil *taken from the two mounds, we*
have concluded : the amount of phytolithic matter, its residue
and imprint, taken into the mounds from the surrounding
swamp and marshy land, did suck plant matter and other soil
subsidations in from as far away as the upper Caucasus.

Silica present in both mounds yielded an elaborate mapping by which both cultivated plant as well as migrating plant (e.g., common sedge) made tributaries and fluvial traversings into the composition of the mounds.

There will still be carbon dating that parses our findings further, but the essential composition of the mounds is divided into two main phytolithicly based decisions. Those decisions rest in the cell-structure of near and far, as well as the essential characteristics from the importing peoples who constructed the mounds.

The ritualized nature of the arrangement of the findings, coupled with the soil analysis, shows two different types of royal lineage resting in the remains:

1/ the plant silica from further distanced regions could only have been introduced from the time of the mounds being first formed.

and

2/ the plant silica, bonded more closely to the remaining silicon dioxide, found in the many layers of sample we took from the site, are embedded with still intact morphologies. The shape or impressions of plant xylem still present, shows there were many non-metallic, non-lithic weavings of local, indigenous plant fibers available to the mound-builders.

Neither one nor the other kind of soil composition will ultimately, I believe, determine the total use these mounds were meant to represent symbolically. The social implications may be relative to any or all social hierarchies. The wash of that terrain is seen in overlap to the present terrain, no matter its many changed features. The fact that there is almost an equal abundance of both types of phytolithic assembly shows that the relationship between one ritualized use over another leads to a mis-interpretation of the basic symbolic contents of the mounds.

Two mounds show a sedimentary horizon that is in some way very impoverished of species composition at about 10 meters depth. Certainly, the tillage of soils in the 4th c. BCE is to account for this, and that horizon line certainly leeched the soil composition as a result. But the symbolic relevance of these peoples and the absolute cross-fertile relationship of the two mounds cannot be shown to be anything but a people's two mounds, used for burial. Interment shows that all the design elements, without question, originate from the same people.

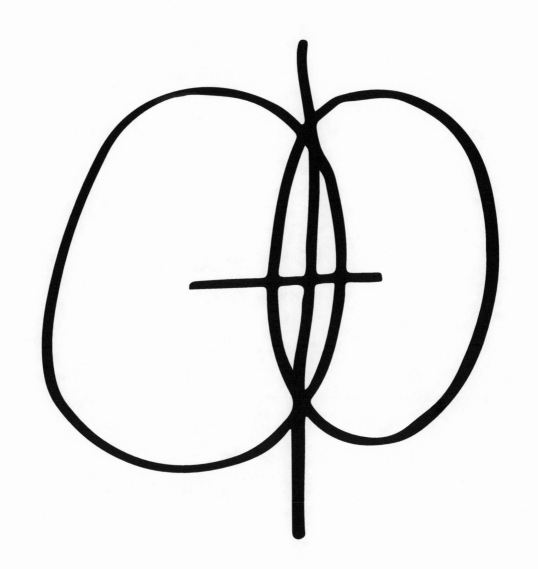

INTERVIEW WITH A REAL-LIFE FAERY

"Observe the landmarks well and I will endeavor not to leave the vicinity," said Don Quixote. "I will take care to climb to the top of these high rocks to watch for your return. But, best of all, so as not to miss me or lose your way, you should cut some branches from the many broom plants that are about here and strew them at intervals along the way as you go down the plain. These will serve as marks and signs by which you may find me when you return, in imitation of Theseus's thread in the labyrinth."

"I will do so," answered Sancho Panza.

Cervantes, *Don Quixote de la Mancha*

"…Daedale Earth…"

Spenser, *The Faery Queen*

*I*caught up with the very old, still sprighted figure, just outside La Venta, Tabasco. We convened in conversation about the change in poetic rhythms, beginning in quantitative into iso-syllabic measures of a by-gone era. In order to enhance our understanding of the fossil record. Our meeting place was a small township near La Venta, a saloon/restaurant with nicely swept stone floors few tourists know of. One of my first questions concerned the geographical locale, which had at first been a surprise to me, noting the return postage mark on the letter received in answer to my request for a series of interviews.

The letter, and then the series of emails from La Venta, however, were received when I'd already been dispatched to the Yucatan by the editorial collective ArcheoOrg.org. My time was spent sightseeing and wandering thru ruins, both on and off the main routes, in order to understand why my communications with him had begun not so much over the ruins and the burial site and mounds of the Olmec, rather, it was the use of a certain tomb or coffin that was supposed to have housed a portal to the afterlife.

The sides of the stone container were braided with carvings of rope and jaguars with open jaws. We joked, or rather it was he who joked that what looked like a coffin was really a bed and that it was probably used, or thought locally for many centuries to have been used, for different orgiastic ceremonies. The open jaws of the jaguars were portals that showed the limp child who would be brought to attention by what was performed, right in the coffin or stone container, making it a sacred, life-giving site.

But before I made my way toward Campeche en route to La Venta, I flew into Cancun with my notes from the previous expedition still fresh in me, tho it had been more than a few months past. I wanted some sun and ocean, so I brought my notes there first. Then, to take the bus west and south at a leisurely pace, before the appointed meeting outside La Venta…

1/10/20__

jj makes me question all my desires but that doesn't mean they are entirely negated.

My look into these questions is enhanced, made whole in a way, relayed and transferred into the world, without any one set formula, by a patience with all things.

And I, partner: there isn't any deeper meditation. Instead of frenzy, a sometimes hysterical mind, I take into the future a rendition of what's to come, after what *is*, for sure, coming my way.

Not just patience, but the full-on appetite for jj as a person. And pursuit of personhood calls my being into question.

I am not questioning myself in order to eliminate myself, but to understand and then enhance my own drive. To refine.

My desires are so much more focused because of this presence— so many miles away now—and why I am writing this paragraph, trying to connect, just a few moments ago, a blissful thought I know could have only happened because of this presence in my own life's trajectory (like the fully occupied plane's take-off and landing).

1/11/20__

Waking up in the hotel in Cancun before heading, on the bus, to Merida I felt the presence of you in the form of the sound which is a way of saying that you, jj, are the *conveyance of sound*. This can be vexing for a moment, but if I stay with what that moment means to the future, to all moments, then I understand how this new body will be joined to its missing parts, re-atomizing itself.

I think this occurred from realizing sound, or hearing (to be more precise), the gateway to sight. I don't know exactly when this happened—and certainly the dream last night, kind of a nightmare, awakened within me the sense that all must continue from the form of my own isolation.

But I'm not isolated as I left with N. who is beside me in bed, lying here now, breathing. Listening to her breathe, my legs wrapped around hers, in the sheets. A trajectory of sheets.

In a dream I was shown who I am. I cannot have access to the intellect. It's that simple, this human person. In many ways, the isolation or exile would come to seem, from my being a form, not a person—I mean some kind of separation between forms and persons.

The presence of the physical body. We know it's a body, of course, but the most important aspect is that it cannot be in two places at once without becoming one of the other, I mean one *or* the other. Integrating the Other into sight.

So hearing was the occasion for language, sound, and also the flight of sound itself, given to these moments, a temporal outlay the sight of things cannot at all *think*. It's evident hearing is a different kind of thinking. Not just thinking, a whole different world, one we cannot really speak about in the normal round of conversating. Something comes into us that calls us away—in order to join it— there.

I was taken out of the dream into the waking moments of my waking self and realized what I heard could have been the birds. The voice in my head talking talking talking (about everything.) And in that speech I began to see: *you*. I immediately recognized your finger and how it was also the groove it found sliding up and down your own groove. This was also the spread open legs which were sheathed in dark black socks, as I also recognized your black hair. You were masturbating, but the groove of you was also the hearing. At the same time, I realized the world we share. Had this become some sort of investment I could share only with you thru sex, thru private rubbing? The dream is skin?

My mind is only to be used for empicturing you in the throes of pleasure—or the drive to meet it?

It's the meeting place of bodies that hearing conducts. You exist in me thru the many ways I bring myself over into you. It's been this way from the first, not just because of sexual fantasy, nor the desire that might stir up in my organs, but the writing, and the speaking to and for one another, has been on the level, has maintained itself thru touching one another. Rubbing up against the other—*there*!

When you communicate, always be this realization. What have I invested in this body? Dreams which you can't help, or you can, because one "sleeps them off." *That doesn't eliminate them anymore than the sleeping eliminates this realization.*

I'm not going to be able to write a history of the relationship the body has to modernity, that seems an utter waste of time. Yet it illuminates the entire reason for every existence. The point is, I am not part of any of that anymore. I actually realize or see the body. Here it is. It has evolved. The same way a groove becomes a growth, a protuberance.

My hearing is the product of seeing, investment in the body, why I am not part of the intellect, or more accurately, an intellectual community.

It's not just that I wasn't educated or groomed to become part of that competence, it's that I wanted to be competent in *another* way.

I wanted to be able to hold myself open to myself.

Everywhere, this realization does open, I begin the connections to competence, performance, not as something to be attained outside myself but *of* myself.

I come to you, and jj, in the form of all of me. There might be multiple bodies, but they are now moving toward you, all the limbs whirling out from organization at the center of the place I formerly occupied. Touch brings all of them.

In my empicturing dream—which fell into hearing this morning—I realize you are always going to mean the way I am.

What conducts my drive back toward myself in its forward moving, or rather its falling forward thru the representative figure at the center of the place you *do* occupy?

And oh how I "need" that forward, to move back, onto me, *where I am.*

All the silly idealizations of sex and gender are only that: ideals; completely unattainable. Yet, you are not unattainable. I was not unattainable. We are not unattainable in this organizing magnetic fall-out, this exile and attraction.

You were offering yourself to me by the groove … the sweet

grooves of "you," and I heard, I took you in as the cognitive form of hearing itself, a path for each and every limb to enter. Each and every investigation invests itself thru me.

Do you understand how all of what we've written, all of what we've conversed and communicated, simply a way to become the brain of hearing itself? And that brain's housed in our skull?

There can be no more visual ideal, or, I mean, no ideal whatsoever, without the moment by which we hear each other: the moment we turn to hearing, here, thru the ear.

1/12/20___   Hotel Caribe   Merida

A moment on the bus ride over here from Cancun, I felt like the arrival of jj in absence, *here*, become a flourish of the arrival within my bones. The distance can sometimes be heard in radio communications, out of voices that talk about local weather, overlooking one's particular place while not being in place. *Within.*

This takes, now, the full expression of all expressivity.

I mean the sun so warm on me on this upper deck of the hotel, overlooking the very old cathedral, not only the sun but the arrival here. The myth of the feminine as well as the myth of the soul mate arrived within us. A time which is rising, arriving.

I see the moment as nothing, concerning the arrival, self as an individual, more than before. Nor am I any less than before, even though what has happened has happened. The world recorded that happening like it would any number of crocodile events.

I, who consider the moment, having felt its arrival from the full flowering intention of jj, in and of the tent, moved with a passion for bones and archeological measurements of the mounds—deliberation toward the "self"—hovering (below me.)

In a similar way, he imparted the moment to me. That is, he is the opening *fosse* by which I am released into sight, by way of the conveyance of sound, whose recordings have already been made by the world, for the world's glory as the world, as the Earth, as it is the eternality of itself.

He—gives me myself, in the form of this momentum, which can renew itself by his love for me in the org-anicism of all bodies and beings.

My love is part of this same birth from self's intentions, to strengthen within, to own loves and interests, lovers and instigations. He, who the otherness of I, sight now becomes in address to you with a voice out of the old time now done.

I can finally articulate what it was he had been so afraid would become of articulation itself: the stickiness and *cul de sac* of the expression, a one-way love that sets itself up against the recording world, positioned in the I as a denial of the participation of all bodies.

The *orgy* of the longpoem.

We have an expression now which is two-way, for the unfolding of *all* ways: our desires never left to non-decay in the vapidity of big D desire; universals that never know the moment, the turning moment as it turns to the recording world, whose images and voices flow from the intimacy of all sensation at the center of a centrally archived writing; the practice of which moves mountains and situates earthquakes and fault-lines, re-envisions laws and re-states their once firmly stated beliefs.

I turn.

He turns toward me, but not as a way to interrupt a movement toward jj. To use me as a kind of incantation meant for me alone—jj, looking for the moment, turns within all contemplations, sees the resemblance ignite the edge of the world's recording voice, *in him*, *in me*, and *now us*.

His movement forward was a sweet movement toward matter, joining both of us with more than us.

jj was not out to re-materialize a relationship toward an end or containment that closed and shut itself up from the world. To relate any world by the fact of confinement and that fact alone, never. In fact, right now, he's waiting for it to open and I know, as the sun casts a shadow over my pen here, dear light is about to explode within him.

I am calling to you in a fantasy of the moment—the exact same that occurred to me on the bus.

The recorded world became other than fantastical, became real, as real as the symbolic nature of the real can be. I felt the arrival of a woman's, a man's maturity. And in that maturity I've been sharing the arrival, waiting, cultivating it within myself and for myself.

But that self is no longer, having given its all. Waiting has been so much pleasure; sometimes I had no idea what I was supposed to be doing. Was I supposed to put on makeup, or shop for clothes in a different way, that is, mindfully? How silly all these pronouncements now seem in the face of this one turn thru all matter by way of the recorded world. Queer—before, during, and after.

Yes, of course, this is a universally human moment, but also one that can take on such variety and divergence of expression it gets lost and forgotten, becomes dead language, reminding me once again that all human kind's personal bests are almost completely illusionary. Objective as they are objects, and dirt, Earth, the profound implementation of writing itself moves beyond, always.

Dirt, the distillation of the world's voices come to the entrance of matter, universal matter.

It's strange to think of turning toward fantasy as somehow different than illusion, but that is something which speaks to the very heart of matter, an elementally erotic feature of form, matter's incestuous family member.

Big "heart of the matter," like a two-ventricled, decorated set of jicara gourds.

I mean the gentle insistence that all of our knowings, our intimations of knowing, are completely gone and have been abandoned to this turning eros, god of every sublated movement.

I would qualify this "gone" sense as not something evaporated, rather firm, solid, the mass of mass itself—for which blood voices its throat, conduit for every urge, translating it as world.

He's smiling now because he knows the absolute meaning of virginity, that movement toward matter—probably the very first true question I had regarding him—now elicits fantasy-vision as an answering angelic, undercover.

Things are combined in matter, and as he will also say, they are combined, wrapped into the cold past, needing it at one time because he is always overheating.

The rendition of the compact, the coupling, the essence of the solidity in both ice and water, the melting and the frozen.

Outside a discussion of metabolism, our articulations understand that cold place. It was the first time. He took me and all my values, and knew they would forever come from that cold place, by that taking.

There's a work ethic on his part regarding this contemplation of my cold emanation. In one way, I am very hot; but that is only one way, that is only sexual dynamic for which I have no control. It is only one way which ends with me, having used up all my resources. It is he who knows the resource can never be un-identified. Instead, steady cultivation of movements, back toward coldness, retrieved my one way, *in*, as many times as it can be retrieved.

I rang him on the phone one day after work, and immediately blurted out, "I can't cum anymore! I feel like I've just spent the last year and a half in the throes of an orgasm the likes of which have never happened before! I'm exhausted! *Where are you*?!"

And that long distance call was like ...

6:00 p.m.

N. and I talking in the Zocalo about the changes in one's own life—both of ours—and a guy starts chatting us up about the weather and whatnot. My Spanish isn't so bad but nowhere near N's—and then he begins talking about the Mayan museum not far from where we are sitting. Obsidian, jade—imperial jade artefacts, replicas of Mayan pieces from Palenque and other places around the Yucatan.

He's talking about amber, too. Es como Copal, I offer. Si, he says, the spiritual part of the head (he meant also the _____) and he puts the hand up to his head and starts talking about Rojo Amber.

Then isolates his left eye with his forefinger, up the center of his nose. On the left side is the material side, investment in a material-ity? Or is it the right side? He's saying one side is spiritual and the other material. I'm getting them confused, but his left eye, isolated, as he goes on and on about the nature of Amber and Mayan art … and at that point I start to feel a very warm wind rising up in me.

He's staring at me and I feel like I've heard enough.

11/13/20___   Sabado

Facing south this morning. Looking out over to the Cathedral. Last night at one moment, the moment I've been talking about and waiting for, carried again from the façade of the Cathedral, as if sex were the first carrier of the trajectory which seeks to defeat all "projections."

We had walked up to the wall to see shells embedded in some of the mortar. Fossilized forms bore an imprint in 16th century mortar, made and baked into place by the Spanish, Christian conquerors.

To hear the birds in the morning, now looking out at the sun, a perfect circle, I realize the directions and that I've been staring straight into the south, as if to keep going forward I have to travel that dimension to encounter the recording world which writes the cosmos into its coming into being.

I had talked to jj, or it was a premonition of all our letters and talks, telling me we have this dimension in the future, where all the souths can come into us. My own walls were so tightened before I met this particular order of non-quantifiable beauty. The crystalli-zation of quality, of the beautiful, in the windows and walls of the Cathedral I found in my fixed eye-sight last night, somehow inherit-ed from the slaughter, battles and eventual conquering of the Mayan order—and there was a drowning wave of release only our creature could know when he comes together out of the cosmic pen—and I've now become his very own mother too as I sit and write on the roof overlooking the Cathedral.

My love is so deep for him it takes all of me. As if I had only seen myself as the wall of an interior, spread over a very small portion of the world, he lets me freeze.

The world wasn't even known. I had never come to the acquisition of his mobility of many selves, all of them unaccounted for under this sun. Identities, I wanted to say to him in my half-sleep this morning, my legs wrapped around N.—all identities come and gone in the approach of this fixed place. Fixed into the star of a frozen mntn I want to show him how every ideal is nothing when not compared to the moment.

This isn't a fantasy of some era, or trend, but something which can arrive and shape us, until we can't really understand why we weren't on our way into the south to begin with. All of us together.

But we are going south, and always have been. That's the sweet transition thru me into the man, in order to find the physical love and necessity, which tells the directions to come into cosmic cycles of matter.

Not just abstractions of identities in a myriad pattern without any subjectivity, but the kind of blood that spurts out from the sun.

The character of the objective, not an abstraction, but a full rounding body that knows each other body, notes the form from without with the forms of one's past, forms internally sealed in an arctic magnetic retina, voices alert and drawing script, recording every new entry as if non-puppeted, an ingestion of matter, winding thru a labyrinth of the body.

Bring the internal relations *out* so they articulate *in* a larger body; of many, not just one isolated, sublated body, called upon to perform as per formula already known and passed in judgment.

All I've ever wanted to do with writing and poetry was in this: come out of some form, some discipline of form that did not need one "thing" to measure, to feel and see the turn into, not just chaos as un-measured expanse, but the varied intensities of forms which will never be able to be re-contained or re-packaged as a marionette of form.

These are necessities now, these ejaculations.

I am unearthing, and in that release, the sound, yes I have a central fantasy of giving all my tongue to the recording wind. It's coming out of the mouth of the ice-cold sun.

The soul: can it be accomplished by collaboration, by marking collaboration into a much more vital response to all intimation, even rumors of touch?

I've wanted to take his arm in my own and feel the reaction, however slight, and show every instance of the cold essential sun-spit, vitally important to the continuation of the web, spun by incantations of the white and black eye of all of us.

To become the wall of sea-shell mortar, becoming one another thru gates of the recording world at the change-over to its silence; never separated, always in patterns of sound, our era, a duality of subjective announcements that forever tie us into the direction of the Southern Matter.

Our memory of the South I have in offering to him that northern validation of his birth.

We know where it is and why it appeared to us thru him and his reach into my existence, an actuality that does not argue from doctrine—the reason coming to us from necessity, just as the poems and the singing are this intense love for one another, this feminine care, enabling by caress we charge our throats with cryogenics.

This change the change in the moment of distance, separation, momentous touch.

How much can I fit inside, so that time will never again want to not write me as its mother.

I want to become his mother, give birth to him, nurse him until grown.

What if he becomes a man one day? Would this be the vanity of my own upbringing, working thru an exemplification of man? Can a mother show the blossoming what the father means?

How do we forget our movements and moments when we take on different roles? What can be unearthed to restore those moments in role-playing?

Should we inhabit role as if to merely subsist? Or are we meant to wake into that role and discover the mother in throes of ecstasy, not an ideal ecstatic, not a touristic fantasy of the role, not some lurid fantasy which has no way to continue in the flesh?

So I have changed from being mother into father. Those warm words that comforted a form she went to become, or touch and know.

It wasn't so simple at first all these break-thru's toward form, love, the incarnation that could re-figure times and eras into blood.

Menstrual perfection. Cells collecting all of us into hips, breasts, the many breaking shapes of body, then to become something not so much worshipped as wondered at, our own blood breaking down, destined for the ground, the land.

Some distant revelation was entrusted to these forms, shapes, characters. Cell-life, before we came, the un-fixed relationship of them. Mind was something never tied down, never caressed or brought to moan. Mind was always in the objective mobilities of time and never in the actual cell-life which works to get thru to the un-fixed moment, to align with it, exchange with it—the opening of which, taking whatever in, whomever wants or needs, an unfixed state—to come and never leave. Come forward.

Strange, in light of the fixed and un-fixed, I see math and mathesis as imperfect relation, consonant to cosmos; and the seeming irregularities of language, perfect, a stolid very decorative absolute, a communication that has little to do with communication, more with fixing arguments, fixing relationships into a fantasy of the perfection of unending design.

Fantasy journal, based on what is dying, encountering entropy in mental empicturing by way of phantastically surrounding space. Everywhere, a kind of nothingness, relates to our/my fantasies of consummation.

————

They sell these little red and purple plants on the streets here: I want to say they're onion flowerets. They have a sharp point and are in clusters of three or four, edible, wrapped up for buying and walking around with, a snack; reminded me at one point of the attachment to jj, simply because there are two ways in which they appeal.

One, they seem so tender like a flower but another is that they probably taste a little rough, as well as possessing a saliva-producing component. The tame and tender quality of all these people and positions, jj is to me. That he has enabled a kind of affiliation, collegial, familial, to be for one another, without fiery and sensual qualities alone.

But there's the very important form of us together as anima/mus to any flower or tree or plant or botanical come alive in the world, in time, in the night. This feeling alone, which reaches out from my physical bearing stretching into you, wanting to spend time with you … this is a kind of extra-filiation of those understandings cumulatively embodied.

… the warmth from every single cold thing, without which they might become permanently dormant. The desire then to not want the other to forget, and to be there for him, as he is also there *for* me, *inside* of him.

… physically identify it as the extension of jj, and all that extension a probing toward my own center. My center doesn't know itself as receiver but as gift and giver. I offer, as an aggression of my physicality, to jj, the center of that physicality.

I have activated my agency and am only the mobility of what application he brought out in both of us. I am so bonded to you, so materialized here in you.

These moments, which actually bring the thought of previous moments, turn toward real thought, real presence, burning away, turning cold ash.

The streets are filled with a smoke right now: fires the smoke and soot of it moves quickly everywhere in the heat by the winds which have picked up strong now.

I can feel him in the air as air. The thought of these moments— the written figure of the poet?

6:00 p.m.

Nightfall—or is this also one of those terms have only come out of me because of jj?

Sitting here, not venturing much by way of the night, into the little park here, two young, flirtatious boy and girl, on the other bench. Now I'm catching up to them here in the notes, a book about what it not only means—the marble steps leading up to the statue, then looking out at the Cathedral, the walls lit up.

Interiors, where the reader brushes past, or before, I saw you walk into the hotel room, saunter in and open the door wide. I was, or had just explained in a letter, how I wanted to see you.

But not really my real life—to take my writing life, to take all of it and never allow me to look back but thru, is more the point of these entries …

1/14/20__

No hay mucho calor en este horario, y mucho wind, but it's coming from the east, or northeast again, almost like a sea breeze. We're about an hour from the gulf, I think. Looking at myself in the baño mirror this morning, thinking how I haven't seen this person in a while. Of course, I always look that way after a shave, but this a kind of lost time. Rather, I was lost in time before this time. Likewise, thinking the name of the maid on the tip envelope is *Yoli*, but I was seeing *Yulia* in the shower. How that moment of discovery, these little discoveries—especially the small—joins me to those times when his voice was coming at me over the phone.

The first was so dear, this voice, clear as a bell to me.

You can't write about someone this way? Porque? Yoli, a kind of shortened name, version of Jules, or maybe Julia? Or maybe even a shortened version of a Mayan transliteration. The liberating thing is the shortness, so young and cheerful, turned up around the edges of phrases as if smiling, but in earnest, not fake or phony.

I walked out into the dark backyard, to be as private as possible. K. had just come home. But it wasn't to hide anything, even though

I had just balled my head off. "Let it come," jj said. Then, later, he said my tears were beautiful.

My god, I typed back in an immediate e-mail response, *I miss you already!*

I remember screaming in my skull at having written that. All of this from the pure pleasure of meeting. Voices.

To follow, sometimes more important than leading.

To be original, often times not as forerunning as you might have thought, when the haunt of genius or these kinds of persona-plains, make a direction for work. But work is work, it has to be done, and you have to do it. When guided by the work, the work becomes available to many different as well as refined perspectives.

But you can't get there without a guide. You can't make everything come from a person or station that only materializes as a follower, your own innate following self in the shadows, the society of that self. I'm not following the idea of person, the personality of jj: I'm following many movements he evolved for himself. Movements only I can see. And in that *seeing*, I become dis-lodged from all following selves. The single-file ends and the group-dance begins, where and whenever it has enough impetus to begin.

I was allowed to become whatever I needed to become, in order to see or to hear.

The change jj embodies in this seeing double, as if for the first time, the world doubled.

The change, a desire which manifests devotion to the matter inherent in the world—not a world of scientific data and that fantasy of mental carnage. jj is on his knees in the shower watching the water fall over the light reflecting, scintillate.

It's a world you would wish to inhabit, imparts another space, the actuality of inhabitation, not merely subsistent, not completely subsequent or submissive, but a response to the initial, preternatural moment the doubling occurs, dawns on one's self.

You have to open the door, you have to let in the time you've been given to write; this is true now, but also from this self in its shedding share writing rituals overlap.

Clear images from the first voice into the second.

How the circle of his beauty, all the way up to his head with the sprouting black mane, dark eyes that change color, his tender cheeks—a movement of one extension for walking, flying.

Poised for *the* flight really, arms as wings, in the offer to me of all these memories, which are all of us together.

It means a deepening forever. It means your many voices.

———

The interest, not so much for people past or present, but in the putting of past into place, where the present can easily put up with anything.

So the past contains many things, yet the present contains only some, held and separated from others on into the future … an incomplete and ongoing work.

If we could come together, the difference between two places would really cease to exist. But how bring all three of them together: past, present and future?

I want the discussion of my own potentials, and all they mean, particularized? I can talk very scientifically about particulars, about actual things, but it amounts to nothing if all I am doing is putting those relationships, those subscriptions, extensions, back and away, into the past. And yes, it's necessary to have a past, to realize one has moved on. But how moved on and why? What's the purpose to moving on?

I am not moving out of any place into another place as far as the vitality of things are concerned. When totally enrapt of terms and voices which have gone, then I feel I have moved. I am neither in the present so completely that my words, my voice now as it comes thru to me, are nothing more than sounding planks for the echo of a dead thing between these two, past and present. Two kinds of lives as well as two kinds of deaths, just at the moment the future arrives.

jj was the first to actually want to be with me. To be with me in a voice that is the accomplishment of an unfolding between worlds.

A real future, not a pretend one.

The voices allowed us to access the center of mutual abilities, of songs which filled the moment those voices … recorded the heart's delicious announcement: you are grace, the moment of a larger fulfillment; desire had its way with both of us, in the sleeping captivity of us til now, friend.

Each body, stolen by wanton deliverance of words, given over to this medial paradise at the whims of names. This was the foundation to the past.

I say paradise because it was a place within which we wanted our own self to occupy and flower. My heart filled with song, an actual pressing feeling upon my tongue. I named my heart a tongue and offered it to the future.

We can never leave this heady agreement because we've understood, before coming together here, abject prayer toward/from our own being as access to higher altitudes within being, approached the present in the form of all of those beings.

This time, given to us, yet together, we can see a greater awareness. jj presses over onto me then too, as consciousness, after full realizations in the solar plexus, drives and self-offerings, sacrifices of song and word drive me for the loveliest engagement I've ever been entranced or taught to be at peace with.

This love has a white, searing mark across the black face of all stations and entrances. We've decriminalized the very enterprise of giving, for another's altitude.

1/15/20__ Lunes

As I was thinking of jj last night, intimated presences, he coupled with the visitation, as a way into consciousness. Consciousness itself as that act and activation site.

Very large doors of the Cathedral we had walked thru—N. and I—but I was a little afraid to stand directly in front of the Virgin de Guadalupe while a woman was kneeling at her shrine. I told N. if it were any other day but Domingo, we'd be able to walk thru-out the

Cathedral, to look and gawk, but not today. A man came up to us and told us the Cathedral was of the Franciscan order, so therefore the simplicity of the shrines, which seemed odd because they didn't look that simple, seemed instead like many elaborate figures against the walls and great wooden benches between huge columns, flowers and colorful manger displays up at the front of the Cathedral, alongside another two rooms where altars and priests were conducting other Sunday services.

So we heard from N's friend Estrella about the Mayan caves near a cenote and other archeological remains, fairly unknown yet available. We walked a few blocks over to Calle 60 en San Juan Park to catch a bus to Opeichen. But I wasn't sure if this was the same place Mayan labyrinthine ruins were and that we had heard about.

We took the bus anyway, thru streets and then out to Opeichen, about 30km south of ciudad centro. When we got off the bus we walked to the end of a road, a kind of turn-around, with open fields and a large edifice that seemed abandoned. A family outside their house, across the street at the dead-end turn-around, making roast chicken and spicing it and dividing it into plastic bags. We asked them about the Cuevas de Maya, but they had never heard of any. One guy sitting there, fiddling with his smartphone said, There are plenty of stones around here which are Mayan but no caves as far as we know. We all laughed.

N and I started to walk back toward the bus stop. We asked a couple of men with their kids and wives all preparing watermelons and other fruits and vegetables for sale out of the front of their house, loading the bed of a truck. But they had no idea where these Mayan caves were we had heard about. So we took the bus back into Merida Centro, and to the hotel room. Turns out there were ruins, just in a location east of there.

I'm looking at the sun now and the sky has fewer, in fact, no clouds today, less wind. I used to tease jj, calling him tiger. He loved this name. I think of him now as a tiger, upholding my body as I sit and ponder or look out of this body.

Everywhere I walk, I seem to be waiting for him to pounce on me out of—not the past—but the fact of things: shadows the sun is throwing out across the tile floor by the pool here. He was the first person to take all my little things and make them big. Of course, this was what I had only let myself discover thru association to him. But then there was a change and it didn't matter what or who the poet was anymore, no longer a relative of the man I once knew in the dream or drama of poetry as chorus, nor anyone I'd ever known— yet not a stranger.

I've certainly seen tigers before, but when you have the tiger so close to you, able to discern all your beliefs, you begin to know what is dear about the name *tiger* and how sleepy you might be without that dearness.

Then N. and I took a cab to her friend Estrella's house. The day before, N. had an incorrect address and we were knocking on someone's door in a western district. An old man answered the door saying, No Estrella aqui. He offered to call the number N. had on her but the number didn't work. Anyway, we walked over to the next big avenue and flagged a bus down, back into ciudad centro.

Yesterday, we had the correct address and so we took a cab. Estrella showed us her paintings, at least the few she had still in her possession. On the walls of the living room she had painted RAMA RAMA KRSNA around a print of presumably Krsna and other Indian deities. Anyway, we lit a bowl or two and talked as the sun went down. A newer neighborhood, maybe 25 years old. The house certainly looked newer, with a little car port entrance, nice tiles and pretty clean it was in general, the street out front. We were talking about lots of things, but Estrella also went on about her ongoing politics, how she ran for local position and was defeated. Estrella's father, in the 70s? was governor of the Yucatan, but had been assassinated. So her talk would go in and out of that time, the time of the assassination, as well as this new time.

The word *corruption* is used for a host of things, but it's obvious that the disappearance of many people, in Mexico, is part of what is changing, occurring from out of a general wave of change which really is centered around the movement of people from South America up toward the U.S., then into the U.S. So the need to stay on the same page—500,000 people moving into or towards the U.S. every year as a unification of many bodies—coordinates the economies and the politics of Mexico, not to mention the interest in large herds of bodies in general.

When the president says maybe there was fraud in the most recent election, for example, the next day people are killed as a message to him, so he retracts the statement.

The masses are all used in every form of communication so that particularization can never penetrate them—they are all surrounded like a caged block of …

So the positive, people, politicians, even vendors on the street tend to revolve around this sense of time, the movement of time toward trying to get money, a better way of life, any kind of security. The desperation it breeds is dealt with brutally, without any policy or particularization at all, as if all the bodies were wanting to annihilate one another in their present mode of organization. As if consciousness has to snuff itself out. Death as censor.

An orgy of killing. But there can't be any policy or way toward co-existence. Even then, the possibility of merge; yet everything is all about police and policing. So this is what begins to enter the thoughts when one is thinking about the world, not just Mexico or the Americas. To that end Estrella was talking about how her neighbors were broken into by the police, their house burglarized by the police. And there was very little to do by way of reporting the police for confiscating materials—computers etc.—when they claimed it was for an ongoing investigation surrounding a missing person or persons (the many.)

The *general* idea I'm trying to convey here is that when there are missing economic activities (like bank fraud and other fiduciary legerdemain) then people can also be made to be shadow people, in order to fit the vacuum, the way the activities are org-anized.

An eye for an eye.

———

What, like a little child, chasing after pigeons in the Zocalo, his mommy right there, right there for him and I thought, Oh, how privy she is to these moments, his head turning to catch the flapping, falling pigeon, another one, to his left, his little monkey head turning to the left. She is so nonchalant, so matter-of-fact about the moment, and all the moments—although to corral the kid as he was running away to chase the birds was obviously more of her duty, her role.

So who is she?

God knows how much I am rising thru my own pleasure at the thought of her, not just the thought of a person, but the role too of that woman. Her role, her gender a preternatural position. Which is to say: she shares having a role with my own role. Both these roles, if they are not seen as joining in a mysterious way, are only then roles, costumes, whose repetitive meanings and mirrorings are simply "meaningful"—nowhere applicable but within the outward cast of role-playing to push it onto the surface of everywhere.

I see the outward, in jj, and know it signals, from the point of my own divergent qualities, into the many are in a deeper unity below the surface, my own thrill as investiture, vestment of the role *he* plays.

The fetishizing of clothing becomes an extension of this connection too, a connection which wants to exteriorize the role as an interior experience, dispense with the other—not permanently, but for the permanence of its imprinting onto my interior. Is he *that* form of passing thru me? Is this an experience he cannot have as a role-player? How debilitating to think him not passing right thru me—just as I would pass thru him!

How, in what role, would he take me? Isn't his embodiment the necessity to penetrate my exterior more *within* me, taking my own interior for his, taking it for his own? The thought of changing roles, of jj with vestments, a role like a priest in search of a priestess is something I could then see—if we see these exchanges as a place of ecstatic mystery—penetrates me as I put the role on.

My mystery, in connection, and so these roles as they appear to me, sense whatever intuition they have, to become extensions and conduits for passage into the interior of the other. But he is not another merely because he changes role or vestment, it is the change in access toward the center, the altar's passage portal to mystery that changes.

To assume any of our roles always denies the preternatural role we are involved in, namely, the initial desire or wish to explore the bodies of this mystery.

This doesn't mean I am that role or any other, no; it's obvious who plays what role, from a purely syntactical and sonorous outlay of the next meaning, the moment, which comes first as an easy universality for thinking and for the society of the mind. Later, the soul which needs to feast on all blood—the capillaries rising to seek entrance, to let their blood cells flow thru whatever human—ordinates communication and passes thru all of us.

The flow moves from bird's song toward flap, a gesture for flight, in order to satisfy the primal, preternatural need which first announced itself in direction of the bodies.

We aren't but the centrality of mystery, I had concluded within myself upon hearing his voice. I knew the body by the voice, the way it could be a fulfillment to enter, entrance of my own agency that had come to the summation of mystery.

The little boy turned his head, almost doll-like, snapping it to focus on the pigeon.

tardes 1/14/20____

A load of pink pigs, two levels on a thru-level camiones, just ahead of us on the road south.

―――

Now the peaceful retreat with long-tailed birds, bathing in tiny pools, outside the door to our room nestled back of the road to Santa Elena. A couple trees here anent the patio with a papery bark, peeling back a rusty, hairy kind of bark.

Once N. and I negotiated the car, which N. had conversed over the phone in the hotel lobby to obtain, then guiding me to the rental stand and getting behind the wheel of the Nissan, we were perplexed for a while, having come out of the periferico intending to take 261, but instead ended up on 180 back to the coast. Eventually, N. asked directions at an oil change place and we found the route to get to Santa Elena thru various little pueblos, stone-lined streets with tiny houses. N. then telling me about the various political elections which pit one district or Puebla against another Pueblo. They take it very seriously, she said.

Now, listening to the water falling into the tiny pool outside our room, surrounded by thickly wooded ground, palm trees and other deciduous and flowering trees. How I can flower within N.

The black bird with the long tail feathers is back, this time to be alone with the pool, then another bird, then another in the tree above. Hooting in the distance, and a cock crowing while the water …

If this world is an entrance, then who is it has entered? To re-enact the entry, it seems we are waiting to be given access to *the* site?

These are merely questions, but they come at the right time.

jj was tuning in the day about a minute ago, but that was down within my legs on down further into my feet. The transition from thought into something which has a magical presence, otherwise called a body.

If we've entered this world via the body then why are we still wanting to see each other in the past? But I don't really mean the past, I mean the place that holds our attention, shades us, blackens us a bit, makes us the shadow in order to find the evolutionary path our bodies took? To trace it, to feel the trace. This extension, which makes me long for the entrance more than any other longing, talks to me in multi-syllabic content, a glossolalia of all the various co-ordinates of what was known, so I might springboard to the present.

But all these terms, just like all these genders, these identifications of person and personality, meaningless in the face of every spring, leap, or fall. If I explain what I mean, is it just a way to explain the various switches and signals of all the tongues that use this entrance?

What holds the entrance together, or open, I mean?

You can slide over the human, the length of the extension, and that is enough to establish a connection. Once the connection has been established, then where do you ground it? Do you make a project out of it? There was obviously a time when I was so taken by jj, even the mere mention of him would make me into his project, using all my wordpower to slide down or up the human, to give me access to *his* center.

I so desperately was unaware of the moment, until I did the slide into him—my vocabulary completely dead, and then as I felt that and the encounter of the death of me having left my lifetime, I was given to the populated sweet tongue of his voices.

I tried to call his name in that moment, but it didn't matter because his own words or tongue came out. tt, he seemed to speak *to* me, in another language: jj's tongue calling *my* name too, calling it into shape, calling it to be a real name, finally.

I was so consumed by his calling that I didn't even know my legs were straight, out to the feet, my mid-section pumping to the entrance.

What do we think we know when we form a thought or a meaningful conclusion?

We've come too soon, our bodies shot into a law of one age and they will not return except thru the infancy of our coming—all of this I heard myself say to jj, straight into his ear in another age.

1/15/20___

So much has been only the containment of shadows, each existence a never-ending recirculation of their own pasts, shadows of shadows, calling into one another for this moment, in silence, where all begin to move back against the shadow in an abundant kernel of potential light.

So this is the way you've been taught to inhabit individuality, to engage with shadows, with the thoughts of thoughts, never have a way out, except thru silence, so that the voice might burst open in the middle of all voices, free consciousness toward itself as not a unique singularity but a single affirmation of what everyone is purely capable of uttering.

The merging of time and space have been *taught* to conceal.

The voices could come out of what has a hold on you, but then that moment would be its total elation. Overwhelming.

You need someone else to bring those moments, which have no shadow or underworld, into relation with the many more that are waiting, waiting out *of the shadow in direct relation to the dark echoic edges of their bodies.*

It's not to say a dramatic thing but the sight, last night, of the one person standing under the road lamp, kind of hunched over, waiting for a ride—it wasn't an emblem of the shadow, it was the realization of a person there, the road empty, a night scene. A person stepping out, or in this case just waiting, and it was a person, is a person, so the reality of the existence of self, I thought, who I might be writing to, exists there too. Even here, as we make a way toward the entrance to the site in La Venta, my appointment.

All the stories might be true, or they might be completely false, a kind of hit-or-miss relationship to knowing. *The brain may or may not actually exist.* Time may not have any relation to shadow, only to night, into morning, then day. But what day? Is there a calendar the days belong to? Can they be gathered and collected and placed somewhere, compared one to another? Will we find the calendar at the site? Is it the unconscious character of anthropological humans, or is it merely a fictive bearing the soul wants as it projects from out the explosion of the species within the planet?

To compare what to what and for what? How many artefacts make up the moon-shot that was, as far as all agree, merely an historical event?

I see you have one of these, and I have one of those, says the day to the day. We are different in some ways, similar in others. Yet by night, completely identical, sopped in available light as the organization of us engages bodies into one another, one by one.

tardes

Green on the stones, inside the Mayan edifice, might have been a paint, so dyed into stone, still survived.

I walked into the second room after the open, un-roofed first floor room—presumably the inner room was a bedroom? Standing in it, the ante-entrance to my appointment, as well as an encounter with the primacy of human architecture itself: going underground as the builder builds out from the insect and animal realms, adaptation to night and day and time, circular time.

And they join with other rooms from left to right on the front side of the edifice, a partly reconstructed palace.

The question: which were the south facing steps? And so I finally go to them, making my way around the pebbly ground to discover the ball court, or where it might have been when these palaces and temples were first erected. Something like 10,000 people inhabited Kabah, which means my thinking has them all working at making stone pieces to build or even repair the city. But is it really a city? It has a connection to road networks which lead to Uxmal, so that will be tomorrow, when N. and I go north a bit to find a place to stay, then South to pinpoint the answer.

Two stones, paired to each other, line the field at the top of the stairs—I mean many pairs, not just one pair.

So the archeologists, sifting thru piles of stones which stream down sides of the temple platform, searched first for matching pieces. Later, they would find articulation, the utterance of the tongue and groove from stone to stone, and the uniqueness of each which makes the palace hang in the heights of air, as if it had grown out of the underground like some beast.

This is what I wanted to show you, the kind of fitting that might work, and you see first the possibility. Then the node or nodule of stone somewhere else, seems at first glance to fit that hole in one singularity. It's a shade you see, in the stone, as a hole, or a shadow of something made out of stone. Some are more obvious than others. Walking to Grupo Sur, we stopped to see the lintel, carved with figures, welcoming the intruder, so to speak. But some of the doors are hidden under the rubble which surrounds the site, *one of many*.

The path was an incredible red clay, and here or there stones arranged so you know there was something once standing there. Then, at the end, the picture I want to show you, a God, stelae, or it was part of another edifice nearby, the Dios del Falos, enormous tool.

At first I thought, as N. had said, a monument to maternity. The huge member as if a third appendage, the head still visible, much abraded so that little relief was left to detail it further. We wondered of the story, or I the placement, position exactly there, pretty much southern-most end of the road to Uxmal, penetrating the surrounding jungle.

———

The thing is: if I write about what you know, will it be any different than what jj knows? Is there an exact similarity between you two, a place where telepathy is working, maybe not all the time, but enough time: your twinned signal the first that always is?

But of course differences as well as similarities, exactly like night and day, each joined by the movement of light, forward and back. Many *directions*.

Right now, a yellow bird peeping up a storm at the bathing pool. What an amazing tongue of sound the song. These were also the uses of hieroglyphs.

On the front of the palace a series of very sweet bas-reliefs, one resembling a curling serpent's tail. But the body wasn't that identifiable because it seemed to also belong to a letter of the alphabet, or maybe just another design element that reminded me of something else entirely. Deep in the underground, beneath the temple's surging architecture, up to the apartments on the highest floor.

———

Stones are made into flutes.

I'm not sure of the exact science of this because we are talking about something coordinated 1200 years ago, but to create the round shaft you have to pound the stone with other stones, presumably with other craftsmen, wearing the shape into the stone, back into it, so it begins to be the shape, the pillar next to the entrance, the wall it will sit in, partly as decoration ... but really, anything that permanent should be, from here on out, considered as anything *but* decoration.

———

mas tardes

The light leaving now. Whatever it was, it's now this person, sitting between the world of order and the world of chaos, but it's not that simple.

The complexities of order are joined to the complexities of chaos, and by them a night is born. Who can say this voice is not as real as it should have been, and for what era? What age would this voice ever air itself except yours, like a lonely print, handmade, each blot a night to hem all your nights and bring them to you, to sound them and lay them down in front of you. My tongue undone, many versions of you.

mucho mas tardes

Is it just age?

It might be; it contains a secret; it contains everything.

The past as trace, a world with much connotation, reverberates, it actually makes one giddy and high because of the potencies it can uncover: forebears, regarding the climbing energies, the change in syntactical building, inflections, causes as well as passivities.

Think about this: because the moment the circle has been completed, another age is done, and men who have come out of the dark into the light can no longer go back. They must somehow sense a loss of blood as a loss of virginity, a passage of menstrual time gone. At the loss there is atonement, avowal to never go backward. It is the night.

Yet, backward is precisely where I am going, in order to find the imminent trace—the ultimate connection, the embodiment of you.

Here I am again, writing by the lightless transcription of voices, into voice. From the great well of echoes, into the new age. *Again.*

late

jj to be heard now. The intellect of each passing egg-shaped night, tunes me into your reach, who might adore a body as well as a found figure.

The white and the black both bear toward your arms, into your ear, a wet tongue. Embarrassment, down the turning canal toward home, landing, tempting containment of me by symbolic regimens in the potency of utterance. Bathing self-neglect too, potencies which words alone might choose to hear as ephemeral palace-swallows or fruit-bats.

1/16/20__

If you take these fragmentary histories for all of jj's history there is only the name, your name, to work with.

Could this name be any more a dream in its own attachments,

or is it the extension of not-me, into matter here?

What would love offer at that moment as a greater opening, a larger dilation, a flaming, swelling heart for you to use?

Here, the story of two lungs, nothing more nor less.

———

[…] seeing the edges of the temple of the magician, we had to wait until the tourists, wave after wave, were finally driven toward the second palace of the emperor in order to understand that the central garden in the back was for the birds.

Small birds carved out of stone on the rooftops and the edges to the edifices lined the garden. What was revealing was the style of all these Mayan temples and pyramids, the housings and quarters up the stairs, each cornice with rare intact carving of a curled piece of stone, protruding out and there are usually several of them up the height of the wall.

If this is a chronological extension from the previous people, so named as Olmec, then in what teaching did (does) this architecture pass on and thru time?

These curls of stone are the feathers. The outcropped feather features the interior cubes, whose grooves evoke feather and snake-like pattern, hold everything together. The stone wings, tail feathers, adorn the edifices so they seem to have flight and are certainly the call of the structure out into the surrounding sky or forest, the extension out from any interior the temple otherwise contains.

They seem like little hooks could catch something or be hung with fabric, but the shape as a final expression of the building as monument is one that gives it a movement in and out, a breath.

In the back, a site which features images of bones and skulls. This was next to the Palomar, a celestial center, where the triangular tops of the platform, interspersed with vacant space, look like grids accenting a pyramid shape, a pyramid's steps. If you are facing the surviving edifice with the still ruined steps in the cemetery, you will notice a stone with three holes bored into it, which N. noticed corresponded to the three doors of that structure, or the three structures which are there to either side of those doors.

Some skull faces are on two sides of the corners of the blocks of stone, as if in perpetual echo to the space under the dome of the changing sky wheeling in flight overhead.

——

If you were the King (and I aim to make you one) then you would see the stelae depicting the two-headed jaguar on your very own throne.

My own heart is storied in your position there, handsome features made to wear the feather, everywhere, calling attention into this world, a constant catch to the sudden strike any creature of prey, innate, intuits along the ridge of your beauty, your nose, each feature defining a cut into another world which surges in and out in monuments and erections of breath.

In that other world, you will see how I've cast you in my own being, smoke out of my nostrils, evaporation from my icy past.

——

Is it possible (writing this after a brief showering rain, the wind kicking up sounds like the rain too, the orders of naming, changing) to find pleasure, unending pleasure?

Plugged into the excitement of a range, a place, what comes to you as place, what history is to me?

Back in time, right at the beginning of all time, the release to my own name came with the neighbor who had called out to my brother (to profane this place in my writing to you) that he was squared. *T-squared*, like the tool used to draw straight lines—and straight, even if they get broken at angles—they mean the letter twice in the first and last name as well as the other precision: brothers with the same alliteratively intentioned mother's ear, the one who names us up out of the underground from the previousness of human time. The meaning of the number 3?

—

Is my history long-reaching enough?

jj an immanence, maybe the only color, maybe the red from the caves these painters and artisans scrape and collect for their paints, for at least a thousand years, used in another lifetime as well, where I might be headed?

This one, if I ever lose it, would mean the world to me. The next might also be such as well, it's hard to tell, standing here in the moment of the immanence of all my moments.

—

When I speak of your throne, I wonder at the immense striving out from your princely former world, into king's height?

The penetrating seal of your seat, the interpretation of the two jaguar heads, one slightly smaller than the one with ears upturned, points to either side of its head.

Is this the Queen?

1/17/20__   (before moving further south)

Dream last night of two features: a very young girl, dark skin and very black hair, with a hat, making fun of someone, maybe a tourist, then running away.

I thought, how beautiful. She must have been about 12 or 14 years old. Then, an immediate impression, stripes of white rocks, or the Mayan temple wall blocks, white alternating stripes, and a very light blue. Cooling rocks, building stones, passages.

—

I.

Questions Put To
The Faery at La Venta
(see attached photos)*

When you think back now, how did the work open?

Not only do utterance and composition—fantasy and romance, the finding and site of the findings—move away from one another in the course of social time, they vie to replace one another as well. It's confusing, but that was the beginning of the work: to separate what was joined unknowingly while still respecting the unknown as something straddling the known.

We can't look at un-earthing artefacts as simply material relationships; they have a fundamental connectivity, right through one to another in the temporal and imaginative, not just their "factual" embodiments. Utilitarian aspects, as well, are not simply charged by their relation to fact.

Artefacts replacing a world of fact?

This reflexive capacity is also found in the "frozen" world of art, as if art itself had been put on hold by the limiting reflexion of fact, of one world, found and added to all "found" fact.

The museum I make note of and have brought about in the initial archeo-logic book, *THERSEYN*, embodies humanity's **many** attempts at imagining itself.

Self and society play out toward the mirage of sight and seeing; multi-mirrored, multi-armored identities.

All against the background of a vast and illimitable Earth.

Housing spirits of art and arte-fact the world has ever known, the museum opens its perspectives. Beginning with glimpses of *multi-moded* appreciation of line and color, naming and shadow, the great simplicities of mirrored time—seeming primordial momentousness abounds.

Yet the very number of representatives, whether Gods or Daemonic human assumptions, seems to dwindle to two primary sets of three.

These representatives struggle with singularity and with their dispersal into the coming multi-moded dynamic of a new version of the species human, one *set* to another.

As mirror for one, an angle effecting endless feedback still emerges, even within two seemingly finite sets. Set theory and the iteration of "chaos" are the new opening perspective?

Often these artefacts are thought to "go out ahead" of the present, leaving us in an extincted moment, in between the two sets, the two "eyes" or gamotic capacities. The Vesica Pisci a sacred geometric figure housing this extinction unknowingly.

Contemporary time abandons us to mere "experiential duration." All sides of the coin are examined. The axial place, the body, where experience changes place with examination, with materials.

The quote here from Cavalli-Sforza[1] means to bring up the conjuration where this long archeology began. The *scope* of evolutionary time, the geneticist Sforza is tallying, yields perspective for the history of Homo Sapiens. Evolutionary thinking, in mirror-flashes of insight, triggers association to the mystery of creation for development, divergence, patternings and long-term projections of that particular species.

Not long ago it was thought "content is a glimpse," that the very gesture of creation would be enough to adjust the association of figure and name. Are you seeing in the site an expression of the entire human species?

1   "Grammar is more resistant to change than vocabulary."

Sforza crunched the genetic data and displays, among other things, a picture of grammar as constant strain among very early languaged groups, regardless of anatomical variations or other group-trait behaviors.

Language is more a mechanical reliable than it is an individualist expression. This undermines the search for first things, as findings do also exist on a level with single bodies.

We are always dealing with more than one body, in other words, and to pre-suppose a social order, involved in descendance, from first to more recent, interprets how and why *this* gets inserted into *that*.

Now, this might be completely understandable, but because of the picture of language, back into the Paleo, a very strong surety exists in what we think we know of language: grammar, that part of language which is "hard" and is the tally of very simple denotations and inflections, maintains a hold over animal man, just as it does today.

Softer words, words with variable scope "suffer," or sub-serve through longevity, by practice and then totemic repetitiveness, within the predominate, harder code to all "vocabulary."

If time is some sort of sentence, we could say new vocabularies always form around the enactment of the *entire* group allowed to hear their own articulation. So, *who* does that "softer" articulating?

Within ear-shot the species has a Paleo connection to us?

This movement from *uni-* toward *multi-mode* is borne by the anatomical whole of the parental brood. It redounds to cycles of dialect and polemic: mother and father, male and female and so forth.

The museum exists both as artefact and what is not artefact: some sort of docent's ramble through different rooms of the museum.

This correspondence has been likened to the cultural difference of one *topology* to the next, one geophysical aspect to the next, one political location to an overarching … way of subjugating all community.

By "subjugating" I mean *causing* there to be *any* community.

Community, however, is never adequate to the four-fold existence of its true potential mobility, its innate migratory inclination.

The inability to receive, and then send, multi-modes through a community which subjugates its productions and conforms reproductive capacities toward uni-moded or dia-moded, sanitized hangings within the museum, has had its time in the history of the world.

The changing modality of production imparts to us now a sense of movement which is auto-phoric, self-portmental, a presence formerly reserved for reproductive organisms; the inanity of first world versus third world revolutions as vying for different trajectories is likewise swallowed by the plurality inherent in productive capacity.

All of these approaches toward our own world make the artefact more than just an inhabitant of the museum.

Does the museum house right and wrong?

In the long reach of this archeo-logos, MOIRA stands as marble statuary to truth and virtue. Unloving, in the sense that her internal reproductive organs might have received *some* physical "sentience" in a mythically charged field. Everywhere she sees herself within the museum as the worshipped deity of organization and of truth.

This was the set-up from the first, where her body and her self were needed in order to "show" the correct forebearance of any mental conjuring.

Of course, the opposite is true. Or, she finds herself moved to discover herself as false, her organic self no longer held in the balance of fate. In reality, she is split, unbalanced.

Her "queenly" role is thus a part of multi-moded awareness, newly meeting both its former and its stripped down present, scene to scene to scene to scene ....

Is MOIRA, then, the fate of archeo-logos?

If the four-fold essence of *philo-sophia* were to become artefactual, one of the first pretensions to fall back into the waste all around us would be the definition, handed down through hereditary time: *philo, love, companion* of wisdom in the form of the *found* thing.

Yet the Greek root here is more multi-moded, nuanced and shows us, in the seat of one's own, the reverence for *Sophia,* place encircled and held by *many* strong arms.

The fate of one is many?

Love, borne by the test of what one's self is (under *many* Gods) is carried by MOIRA as a *fatality* of Sophia. This is the "lineage" of thought, that it be held by the appearance of many arms, caressed into the multiply-partnered dance.

Time, too, is split by this dance, as if it were needed as a perpetual "time-out" to the dance.

Moira struggles to get to her feet, to pull on her dress, to assume some sort of previous, some sort of "bequeathed" moral dignity.

In other words, what is held in the mind as one's love interest, one's "Queen," must be tested by the appearance of MOIRA. Just as it was in the first cradle of civilization.

The massive dia-tonic heart attack for MOIRA is contained in the fact that her organs, her organic compounds, are not such an "ideal" validation any more. The nightmare of realization, as if a stone were realizing its nature and not simply its "accidental" form, permeates the very theme of the dig-site.

Hands reach out to her in order to touch her moment, to show her it is just a momentary nightmare. Whether she is brought to "life," or not, is beside the point because that has always been her destiny.

So it is a group attainment of touch, the four directions?

As a figuration of the dig-site's source-structure, MOIRA matters greatly.

I have been at pains to put myself up into these figures, these images, these *essential* names. They are not merely existing, they are emitting and this is my own admission into them. No caricature emerges out the other end.

I've always thought of my *I* not so much as immediate reflection in the mirror, rather, on-the-way to finding itself, the lost yet heightened material of a temporal feel goes unnoticed in the low-ground adhered-to appearances, the common, everyday appraisals.

Out of the dark, the tender manifold?

I know I can and will enter a circular reasoning on high ground, eventually retreating from it with nothing more than image or the imprint of time spent *there*.

Others can form a lasting impression, on into eternity (of that high ground) yet what my *I* comes away with is a sense of the danger of being human homo sapien. Human Being, the future, which is completely unknown, criss-crosses unknowns which lie deep, buried within my own mortality.

There have been core-samplings that radiate from geo-physicality. But the inscription is commandeered by a compositional utterance that is universally immortal.

Our height is the living uttering of *AH*; our low-level, death, unable to utter *AH*. And that, as a projected and projectile, within and without the human, simply cannot be possible at one and the same time. Or so history repeats.

We eat and receive the possibility for our *AH* in matter that cycles out of the matter of all matter.

To think we could *think* the end of *AH* is not at all rational.

And we are anything if not the epitome of rational creation.

Why think *about artefacts?*

The body, Allegorized by evolutionary insight = the Museum of the Genus *Homo*. Or does not equal it, too.

Thus, smaller histories are subsumed under the totality of artefact preserved within the museum.

Even as these artefacts emerge from any new work at hand, Allegory—the ability to change and transpose the shape of story—works as a scriptive device, carrying us through, and even out of, the museum.

The bounds of time and space?

All of these intersections with the long linkage of artefact meet a rejection of the worth or value presented in their place.

The composition of artefact tends toward a previously unheard-of vocalization, a change in the vocabulary of being, for which any audience is only slightly prepared.

Music as gift, no longer gab?

Yet what of such utterance? Does it merely have a life within the social body, whose breath has been temporarily taken away?

Isn't that body in need of being disrobed from the social, in order to allow an examination, an auscultation?

The heart of emerging life-form synthesizes into its own blood-beat?

Museum-quality non-linkages form the births and deaths of a given artefact's social life—*contentions to the life and death still to be consummated* representing the boundaries of a "life's work."

Entrances and exits?

Allegory showed a way of holding, within a proper noun, a potent facilitator for anti-thetical imagination, the as-yet-un-named, stripped-to-the-bare time and space of mental activity the individual was indeed *given*.

To make big, that is, what seems so small and never part of a greater composition, never part of "reality."

Yet there had to be a syn-thetic passage for the proper noun or name to be made acceptable and believable.

Somehow, *realism* always was the merge of phantasy (spelled with a ph) and thought-in-activation, submerging all the species into an aesthetic universe.

It's simply not that difficult to accept early ancestral hunter-gatherers were also consumed by this proposition. They, too, in some under-the-hill momentousness, made connections which pleased their "un-reality" more than other event.

If we figure the rise of language as something fitted upon unspoken life-spans of these Homo Species, even back toward hominin, we find our-selves crossing minds with various forms and shapes and contours in the throes of multiplying, pairing off into safer, concealed places from which to conduct their social organics.

An unconscious urge would be the dance. But to what music?

To copy or imitate shape and form is one function of a rise in aesthetic awareness. It is quite another to *apply* the imitation, to insert it into a real live living being.

Even cliché ushers forth a true picture?

If one stops imitating, there may still exist the predication of those shapes no longer tied to repetition. No longer a reflection that holds it captive.

Among other theories which have taken shape by Paleo-thought, one mentions the appeal stone-knapping might have had as a symbol for signaling the potency of one's sexual stamina.

But by symbolic representation, this theory makes sense when we notice it is not so much what *sign* a thing stands for, rather the *significance* girded in the loins, rises to the power gotten through an advance in knapping stone to a sharp, useful cutting tool.

The faster the hide could be shed off the carcass, the greater the *signification* the tool obtained. The signification was the manifestation of all desires and needs and hungers.

Why is the body clothed in darkness?

Contention is a seed in all things. Contention is planted by lingering utterance that does not want to know its opposing. This is what is true. This is true no matter who utters.

So as we look for artefacts at the dig-site, we try to keep in mind that utterance identifies itself as holistic because it does not want to inhabit the psychic polarity of opposites, of anti-thetics.

A decision has to be made, regardless.

The knot in a tree-trunk?

All utterance sees itself as having escaped the clutches of a systemic, neural anatomy.

Fate brings about a sure-fire end to its pleasureful opening toward its surroundings. This is what we take in when we survey the site: what was given *out* as pleasure. We don't really have to ask why.

Utterance shot out of the predication social, grammatic, stellar and religious circuitry.

Utterance was the product as well as the technology that revolutionized the entire acquisition of the world, revealing the scope of the species.

At the same time, these utterances covered over everything.

When we find marks, we have to always understand they were meant in the covering up of the species as well as the world, and should be taken to mean as much.

Are we dealing with designs or world-views?

Putting utterance into the dig-site, right at the center, imperils utterance and at the same time threatens the compounding Earth with displacement.

Utterance threatens the ruin with ruin. Unless, that is, utterance can be used in conjunction with artefacts, their finding as well as their being simultaneously misplaced.

Contending with artefacts means to find their shallowness as well as depth. We can stare at a frame in the museum until all that meant a depth becomes a ground. The preternatural seeds of utterance will in time spring forth. The battle gives way to a new line of warriors emerging from the scene's struggle.

From death, peace springs back evolutionary syzygy. And evolution is indeed something that is the soul of these artefacts.

We are involved with design, a wrap-around one, as well as an overlap, one that is the world itself.

Is this war work, or play?

No matter the struggle's new moment or insight—brought out from a hidden in-the-open place, or, the dig-site as anatomy, a recognized, assumed body—the evolutionary scope of our species brings its return into form.

To leave this circularity is not possible, except it occurs within the mind which is really just a vessel for the spirit of war.

The soul pulls, if it were a bird, prying open a mussel. Or, as you can sometimes see, seabirds drop mussels from a great height so they fall into the obdurate sand, thud, busting open.

I've never been without the mind at any time in any of these digs. But you can tell by the manner in which I speak, and the way in which the image of me in the field, differ.

As soon as Archeo-work stops, I stop. This kind of resistance from after-hours moonlighting is what's needed to keep one sane. Put your moon in the dig-site, as well as up and down and in and out, and nowhere, I mean *nowhere*, else.

What is time?

The calendars and tallies of old led to an overlay or mental terrain, charting difference through cinematic attention. Image got up and moved away.

Image moved and keeps moving to this day, always rising out of the unknown, and in so doing, confers status upon the static. The movement is not just an upright move toward bi-pedalism, it's more the movement finds itself getting higher and higher, presenting itself as the dream of the species, as opposed to the mechanics of a series of images flipped through.

So animations were really the creation of a blur and are nothing having to do with clarity?

The dream, and to dream ... is the encounter with this vertical movement.

In some ways, time was invented to keep track of the vertical, then fell out of interest in that direction; or people just forgot, and so time just went off on its own from one thing to another. That's the honest-to-god's truth, too. It really doesn't mean that much.

Form-to-form geography seemed to start out, as the archeologist is also doing, from assumed parameters or rates of a time-factored State. But it's not the factoring that matters, it's not the calculations which allow comparison between artefacts, it's the sense that *space* becomes synonymous with knowing.

The Big sky?

Seasons perform or rehearse a re-entry to the covering or house of the human mind. This is a very primitive spirit.

Primitivism is a complicated enigma when joined to soul. Together, they form what form is without time—without the measurement of time—but a time that's come to be *in* their unioning.

All unities come from this very common coupling which the primitive and the soul understand. It's all they know. They don't know anything but their joints, their joining. It's *everywhere* they've ever been.

The future is created out of their coupling. The movement, out of their image as the image of all bodies, engages the same image.

What about the chemical analysis of soil as well as artefacts?

By way of the dig-site, over against or a-slant the more primitive, holistic kind of utterance, the Archeo-worker continues *working*.

The un-attached, un-civilized, non-allegorical and hence fragmented enigma of all systems our holistic pronouncements eventually become, *works* the composition away from thematic embodiment, toward the truer, phantastical center of all interpretation.

I mean the shear phenomenon of all matter.

And this is the point of Archeo-work: not to forward one's own agenda. The goal would be to elucidate the phantastical (spelled for the phantic), and leave all the so-called reasonable assumptions and ideas where they live the most: right where they are, thing-like words, fodder for the grandiose.

Instead, bring the grandiose into its new home: a pile of dirt.

Who creates the view that sees the most-seen things?

An epic which hasn't even begun, an epic of phantasy, the phantasy of interpretation, its trappings, people and schools, all the funders to the museum, purchasers of artefact, make their way out of the mathematical nimbus of recorded time. And look, there too rises the Allegorical figure of "you."

Exits and entrances?

We test our knowledge base by the inherent placement of the words we use. We begin to see our enchained being, straining toward tropism, no longer able to sustain itself by rules.

This metaphor of metaphor, whose nature was birthed by the arbitrary capacity of language itself, must find a way to reason. The worker is anxious to discover.

More often than not, we find the endless differentiated space each word naturally acquires (through the museum!) hidden under the lack of any phantasy.

That is the parameter of our site.

Here, there was the word marvelous, but it has been changed to phantasy, to echo that which is arte-factually, eventually objectifiably determined by us.

Where was language invented?

A necessary addition to what letters, literature and enigma are as arbitrary engagement with its first permitted act, resonating through-out the cellular and organismal nature of bounded and un-bounded living *form*—never leaves the atmosphere of necessity, finds a multi-moded need within short-lived utterance.

It finds a *subject*.

The space for which that subject claims itself as self is really just the same space the coupling of spirit and soul found in their joining.

And if you turn the light off when you're at the dig-site, you're only fooling yourself.

Are you listening to music at the dig-site?

A dig-site orchestrates.

Just as our identities form an actual soul in the depths of historical, preternatural pre and post time—actuating the presence of non-repetition—so too the work supra-enfolds upon itself in twisting, turning forms of itself.

Snake-skins shed as well as the movement of locomotion on the surface of water?

A coordination of overlaps, conducted by subjectivity in the name of an objective, music changes and enlarges the scope of the museum.

Utterance hints at the labyrinthine structure and provides light at the end of long corridors, where otherwise you would hear a pin drop.

Up on the top shelf: that's all there really is left to do: listen.

In music, tone comes to its instrument as to a dumb-found brute, bereft of melodic coursings, straining at the momentary contraption, the wood or metal or even electronic device that gave flight, seemingly, to a world beyond its own.

Within the pitch of the planet, atmosphere as preternatural device comes to a pre- or post-historical world: matter.

An elemental concordance?

Human form rose from the seeming nothing of all material presences.

Gathering essential nothingness (as far as we've been able to calculate and rope in with the forms of our museum-based knowledge) the totality of this or any work.

Procreative impulse to the poetic, out of that nothing, in the form or guise of a sketch ("ANONYXA"), gives rise to the entire area of the succeeding work. A simple moment in *diaresis* (··) denotes, as well as connotes, coition.

She sounds coition everywhere by her subjected matter, her survival of pitch-perfection, something her position or agency will always declare.

Homo Sapiens have even adapted to their *own* adaptations and developments.

Could knowledge have existed—always?

Within the animal human, modified through descendants, who now have to re-discover their own history, so much written by victors as much as by a flat-lining or repudiation, where life is written *out* of all processes.

The dis-continuous doesn't belong to history. Pure and simple.

Diaresis a skip in the groove of old-time vinyl?

History's grammar we learn as emigrants and immigrants. We adapt to the adopted tongue, searching for ourselves even as we're losing or hiding ourselves as elemental creatures.

That's the human condition. It underlines national organization as a super-imposition within the Law.

Are Nation-States only ever Stages of development?

Knowledge is based on a vocabulary we think we don't have to learn even one more time.

Yet new vocabularies make their way into the world.

For this wandering migration, much earlier in modernist time, Jung wrote:

> "Just as the human body is a museum, so to speak, of its phylogenetic history, so too is the psyche."

And this sense of working through the Museum as a re-invigorating and primally engaged student—persistent envisioner *through* assumed archi-tecture—constitutes the multi-modular aspect of being, uttering, digging and discovering. The walls vibrate with echo.

Our histories intersect by way of psyche?

Yet we don't cling to the Self of Psyche because of preternatural or arbitrary engagements with anatomy.

We do not, that is, create an unconscious by way of Law or State-craft.

We only tap into it.

What about Law and the Psycho-logical revolutions? Are they compatible at all with evolutionary descent? Descent, that is, with modification?

Just as utterance tells from deepest wells of neural anatomy, so it perpetuates the *neuro-tic* of its own uncertainty.

Un-knowableness within what we perceive as the super-structure guarding any knowledge base, knowledge's own never-before-measured, fragile and limited engagement with endurance.

Out of which the Tables of Law as well as Taxo-nomic utterance?

We can draw it out through phantasy, i.e., the post-interpretive necessity that exists when time is thrown away.

Knowledge is all-pervading, interconnected mortality. Knowledge is not a dead or completed circuitry of *genus* any more than it might be possible for beings to be gobbled up and owned by any one of that name's *species*.

That's not what genus is as *generator*, is it?

We're always in the presence of *other* sub-species within and without the many anatomies of time, until time goes away.

At which time, we encounter the presence of death.

Time's what is mortal *and* immortal, a death-in-life as well as life-in-death modification. The temporary category we place it on or under, in order to satisfy the nearest critic who has just gotten bold enough to cast the first stone, inscribes the circularity all over again.

When do things overlap?

Something about the self-consciousness of digging—it becomes overly conscious. Transmissions move the neural-optic to inhabit itself with self-created light. Patterns are held within the eye's capability.

Self-knowledge is an illusion, just like the eye itself: it sees but doesn't *comprehend* what it sees. It dreams out the threads it wants to maintain over time, in order to create a correspondence with time and duration.

The eye's knowledge, completely visual, every visualization complete. Related to every other completion?

In digging, where the elements become elemental to Archeo-work, they cease to have any other value outside the work of digging. A good thing too, otherwise the Museum would swallow everything. Gobbledy-gook.

We're looking at the dig-site as a view, not a stomach. What if the view changed? Obviously, the elemental digging could be like a fugue, or quite simply the philosophical enjambment of point, counterpoint, and then resolution.

If music comes up again, does that mean it, too, resembles all other completions?

It isn't that resolution is a cessation of curiosity.

Resolutions find building blocks for expanding. Because of the expansion, the work still has to engage the view.

It becomes another view. Or, it becomes a change, at work.

Multiple layers are multiple visions of the syncretic, and *not* the synthetic.

I mean: not the eye-ball you *think*.

The Diachronic invades the Synchronic?

How does layering know itself if it is only a repetitive act? You are asking.

The dig-site.

The dig-site can only know itself when it breaks out of its theme, counter theme, and cadenced rhythm it thinks it is building.

Spatial Memorizations?

Error is always the place where knowledge, as a fund for the building, exists.

For instance, the ruins surrounding the site we just saw, reconstructed from their extreme ruinated state, are really always drawing on their elucidation, light, the fact that they are leftover, undone, incomplete—still in ruins!

They draw their knowledge from what's around so that design elements, both complete and incomplete throughout each site, form any angle in time like a whole tone does its tonic scale.

The ruins and the dig-site have a kind of visual sparkle to them because they can't be completely read from left to right.

They have to be read, as ruins, from every angle. Including the one just being seen right now.

Is sight a different world than sound?

It was Adam we called when we named—as we did *Zeus*—as we do *Sophia* and *Zoë*—because we are desperate to own the story that started somewhere with someone we see ourselves in the skin of.

Yet nothing could be further from the truth: and this is the absolute projection of ourselves that threads the visualization of utterance.

This idea of being first, to name, is not something to be owned. If so, it would have founded Archeo-work.

That tells you right there, something is being overlooked—more likely hidden.

I would put it another way: Owning isn't or wasn't ever the need to own something already pinned down, like the Earth. Quite the opposite: uncertainty in the molecular, sub-atomic, vacillating abstractions of names, over against the fairly stationary, agrarian places, the place that when planted, forms in multi-form, makes language the elastic realm it is.

That elasticity only lasts as long as the age of "objects" lasted.

We're about to find out what the time of objects finally meant—very soon.

What of utterance as bio-chemical illumination?

Desire for owning endless rhythms and connections is always a curious effect of progress as failure.

Each age has its highs and lows as limits.

Low can always go higher and high, eventually, finds something beneath itself in order to have any place to walk out on. And away.

Proper nouns vs. nouns: can you talk more about the tetragrammatonic effect of time and space? Is it always yin and yang, or, that "the meek shall inherit the earth"—that kind of proposal?

The Adamic figure doesn't name things to populate the world from a sense of being first to inhabit the name, like an inventor.

The invention was got from reaching out beyond any self (hence "the fall") and then all the rest was gravy, the names and the other things that accrued *to* the first.

Anthropo-logoi organizes all bodies in the same way—from that reaching beyond.

The Adamic is a commitment to giving the agency of name—its unconquerablility—over to Eve, so the invention could finally be both seen and heard.

In other words: thought about, savored, held together in taste. Eaten.

If we consider the dynamic of two, this is perfectly in keeping with the sources of just about every idea or practicality—a dialect, constantly incorporating difference from the one.

Is it from or form?

The idea of falling, or of some sort of retardation, is the whole point of the essence of the thinking of the dig-site.

The artefacts keep piling up like so many bodies in a heap.

When we put sexual role-playing into the mix, we bring the specter of Lilith, the daemonic side of Eve, back into biblical terrain as a way to bring in the shadow of what the biblical misses.

That missing link is the birth-site of the Angelic, not a mechanism for inhabiting the projections of *names*.

If you remember, Adam named the animals. He would have painted them on the cave walls too, in order to surround himself with what he was not, in order to take pleasure in their esemplastic form.

The unity, the esemplasticity, is the opposite of inhabitation. The union with animal motion is there—to divine, to guide, to give birth to the "unmarried" side of Adam/Eve.

Opposites attract?

Whether this is a metaphysical frame or not is immaterial. The population of ghosts and figures have nothing to do with the essential projection of life on Earth. They are the eidolons of those ages or projections.

But any knowing, brought through the invention of touch, is not narrow. It is, in essence, the anti-nomial.

Eve's reception, the sound, the spatial localization of both time and place, free play, can call back to its initial, holistic moment.

These are simply ways to isolate the projection and make it unhinge from its "universality."

Intimacy understands what is round and what is square. It's a primary, essentially neutered compound, without the reception being part of the positive and negative poles of a battery.

The charge is everywhere absolute contraction as well as absolute expansion. Our recognitions spark the polarities.

How are the common areas of the dig-site made aware of their living arrangements in the past?

Creation always plays upon the dig-site itself *as* Name, first, then hears itself go through strange associations which only the site—whose parameters are set now through un-named space—holds.

The grand stories or mythic totalities of ancestral identities come not from the ability to reflect or capture the eye's attentions.

Rather, sound, out of the names, incites and wraps its rising on the passing of the words into their past, to be buried in the past.

Earth as conjugal interlude?

If we follow time, it becomes taller. It multiplies in creation.

Fullness to name commingles other sound and other utterance, making correspondence possible.

The heart opens.

The purpose is to find what it is the station of *me myself* and *I* has done to this place.

What of the bodies in a heap? What of the pile of skeletons? What of the remains of their organizations?

When the sources or influences of the dig-site are held in contention to its measurements—different than a critical intersection, rejected outright, barred from the museum—the nature of Archeo-work turns upon that same contention.

Rough seas visited these dried out sites at one time too.

These are then the poles of the work: two ages, both tied into a coupling as a soul meeting the spirit of contentiousness.

Time is now the fullness of contention, ready to explode through the the artefacts. This is the blooming of the age of objects.

The present age?

Indeed, the fact of contention, of war-like stance within a work of art, validates the use of all its parts in a split-second—as if the study of the martial ability of a people is also its projected essence, its spermatozoa lancing into ova.

It is as if completely dismissed, all Archeo-work as a mode for power brings alive.

A strike of lightning bolts through the ways and means of the work.

Charged with power, the Museum could never conjure this kind of activity on its own—unless it were more than a museum and, instead, transformed into a purely political struggle.

Every identification is thus met in the event, the rise toward the hierarchical, which nests in the earliest motility of any kind of "machine," primitive or sophisticated. By machine here I mean the translation of the re-productive into pure production.

Assembly lines and factories seek a need in politics as opposed to polis?

It is a way to see the relation between symbolic correspondences which rise out of the body or the Earth, over against those same symbolic correspondences put into the vacuum-tube of contention as site for resolution.

How can the museum-site be thought a dig-site without this transformation and re-projection of its physical essence?

Isn't culture just a swamp that never stops rotting?

Bring in sex and we easily enact both high seriousness and low comedy and get rid of the pretensions that might still remain in Archeo-work.

What is the most moving part of Archeo-work for you?

The pure cinema of the work is gotten so that image exists, finally, at the center of the animatedness. And then it's time (to leave).

This gathering of bodies is what the hierarchical is for, so the essential movement of gathering can be brought back again to a mechanical spirit. It takes a lot of effort to move, invent the ply, the fulcrum, will, to move the central image as it first had been so moved.

The re-acquisition of the museum happens when admittance is gained by bare and newly stripped down displays of dig-site workers, in other words.

Cinema verité, as of old? Everything old is new again? Peep show arcade pin-hole camera obscura?

The momentary then of such an environment.

The cultural context changed from scientific, medial analogs toward a policing, a cult of all context, a battle-front.

Not "digital," but meltdown. Where's the horizon?

By means of this *policy,* all are charged with the burden of war, which is the only thing that can be produced.

The *solder* has welded *soldier* to citizen as the only means a State seemingly shows wishful, corpuscled attainment. Stages of dramatic change and heightened human pique exemplify the State's recently voided space (the museum before the arrival of the nudists) in favor of the symbols of war's ultimate power: the projectile, the pike, the rattle and the round disk of sun and moon.

How some things never change, I see—but it's that they have emerged in different guises. We just have to find who they really are?

The comedy, the farce of it is easily seen by any dissection of the conjuring the State does. A spreading wide commences, without condemnation. Or, I mean, lack of measurement which invites condemnation.

Say Ah!?

This absorption into war-time policies is certainly the case with every procedure attached to our work's archeo *source*, its diving dance through-out aesthetic discussion: whirling, fevering solo rejections from any part-ner there ever might have been, choreographing joyous protestation in accord with the blare of the stripped down re-partnering battle-scene. At one time, rejected, *all of us*, in the first, the most common instance of it.

It's image. Played to comedic effect.

Image is the primal image by which all places are formed or will be formed in order to move, animate, or, more likely, pretend to move.

Is all making the movement that informs impersonation into persons?

As of this Archeo-work taking place here at La Venta, there are approx-imately 16 to 20 million participants engaged in new War Games, online and at home. Time became the literacy of all war's symbolizing domina-tion through-out that population.

Remember, it was simply a contention which brought the new war closer to us.

If you were to write about this new war-gaming, very little subject mat-ter would need to be replaced in your own Archeo-work. The reality here would see that game in every artefact. Your own boredom dares you to it.

Are you talking about the subject of the work or the subject's working area (all that out there?)

The reason many people see not the gothic in Blake's illuminated tex-tual system, and instead immediately see story-boards for a comic book, now that the animated dimension via the internet's inter-active zone is ….

Applied knowledge entered a wholly visual era game ushers into thought. Which is not thought to be a game. That's the trick!

Gothic, here, may still apply. But what to do with that knowledge of the center, when the access to knowing is being kept from thought and thinking at the prime site?

Could be any age, era, or attendant aesthetic sign, it really doesn't matter. Artefact is this timeless time-piece.

Look at the shelf with all the brands of shampoo. Each brand name has a special meaning. Look at the brand logos. Aren't they interesting to you?

But this is the resurgence of the fact that Archeo-work is not a place for knowledge, new or old, but a place for *reflecting*.

The sidereal rotation of the phenomenal world is a mesmerization thru an all-too-human environment?

Archeo-work is a place for the intrapsychic phenomenon of novelty, whether that novel reflection comes from the social or any other organization.

But reflection isn't novel. It's truth. No?!

Penetration is always the drive of the archeo-psychical and of artefact.

Formally, a mechanics or puppetry of the verbal, it makes the bridge or transformation to an *infra*psychical realm. It is a focusing.

In other words: thinking and thought. Modern science believes, as does religion, the human brain is so immensely complicated it cannot be fully "understood." The absurdity of this belief system is first comic, then greased lightning, then fiction and nightmare.

Informally, through the formality of the dig-site, these psychic infra-zones use whatever tactic or triangulated phantasy to effect infra-sense:

to strip the bodies that intersect the site and add them to the infra-embodiment of the soul's dimension.

The soul itself is the tetragrammaton of Earth Air Fire and last and most importantly Water.

The soul, as it hovers over the dig-site, is reached by the fire which issues from any watered site within the site, any place that might have been used for water storage or flow, not simply the name of god, but its naked re-birth.

Are the primary elements of the universe immaterial?

Time as a novel function, or, what might be real, shows the new use for time. But is this time?

So there is another world?

From out of this temporal acceptance, Dasein became Da-sein. It is a universally discrepant term.

At the back of all my Archeo-work, I have this prime understanding that every form of human projection is the legitimate common denominator underneath the ground of the dig-site.

What's in the ground? Or is it only who?

The translators used a hyphen when originally rendering Heidegger's work into English, while the philosopher used archaic and ur-etymology to re-name the former site of scientific enquiry.

Hated, the spoken has been trampled. Song and its artefact were made subordinate to an ordered and un-classifiable, yet insistently categorical spasm of seriousness—for which modernism shunned half its soul-life.

From this shunning, we have what is left to consider: the industrialization of the West.

Strike!

The procedure itself, reactionary as well as liberal, the inspiration both individuated as well as consolidated, under the drive of the so-called State, exists as unexemplified image.

The burning brand of slavery.

How do shackles hold, even when they are meshed with the competently sartorial?

There is no one, or very few, left to call the State what it is: an empty cave, receiving oceanic thrust and ebb, hollow yet impregnated for a term of time.

Metaphor is used to accentuate the shoreline between consciousness and the unconscious, the future.

Like a punkt or point upon which the entire universe contracts or expands, this is the unconsciously modern use, especially in English, of language.

Language subservient to the central "metaphor."

In the realm of story, are we always listening to something told by the dead, the deceased?

When the nature of the reception of an artefact is banished, repudiated or promulgated by this war-like totalizing affect in mindless (bodiless) gamesmanship, then the choice of source material (adapted or completely original) becomes relative and equivocally answerable to moods and dynamisms spirited and possessed by contention's fraught, preternatural psyche.

That psyche, as the soul of pleasure, seeks a group by which to organize its most elemental instincts and drives.

When a group finally organizes and merges, is it always for pleasure?

Through the psyche, Earth seems like paradise, if only it could be worshipped as emptied of the human.

So the charge of the oceans multiplies as a way to catapult charge into the planet by *infrapsychism*, searching its local habitation, its shorelines.

Meanwhile, the contemporary shine has blighted and blinded even the launch into space with its God-like array of sexless, imageless modernity.

So the beginnings of any Archeo-work endeavors to be the source of life itself. Searching, a span between the two, between left and right sides of the heart … and the human anatomy.

Image is found and stripped and held up for apotheosis. As many hands as possible upon that rising figure.

Up and down, north and south, planetary waking from the nightmare of the rich and pathetic, the parasitical, war-like dreamscapes of the underworld pass away from the cinema that has engulfed all organization.

When I hold "the stick" is it always a War Club? Or does it possess an opening, a recessive alignment by which it more truly exists?

The old saw, Ontogeny Recapitulates Cosmogeny, resonates throughout this very contemporary refusal to acknowledge any one source as the final site and direction of life.

Humans are condemned to hope, to start over, contending with themselves as imageless and thus bodiless, enclothed as if ensouled, fulfilled entities, until they are no more.

The truth of death became the horizon to the empty and the common they think they desire to possess by one another.

Is the naked human figure our truth?

Any approved dystopian material, of course, lacks contemporary appeal. It is so *easily* approved and adopted by a fulfilled image lodged in the mind's place of the body.

Rendered empty, frame by frame, the image, ushered into the center, drives form through its essential conjure, whose voice can now breed.

When we catch hold of reflection, we begin to sound out depths, the recesses of the dig-site already under way. It is the fuller embodied presence which brings the voice to meet the spiritual double, the stripped artefact of the soul, the primary arrangement of bodies, then as well as now.

When did you meet the fate of this dream?

Even to be within one moment of the dream, my life is compounded into a questioning that becomes so multiplied it actually threatens my existence within that multitude: all the threads existence might have gathered are unwound by association.

My associations are not held in a theoretical place alone, where Religion and Dogma, for instance, are held to be "preter-natural," where they never intersect with the present.

How absurd to make dream this kind of theoretical space.

This is my sense of history, and it is why the emptiness of image and artefact cannot be seen as merely fulfilled when they have been emptied and moved to the center. The center?

The empty image is essential, in that it is the source of the projection the artefact embodies.

A bombshell?

The artefact is the reach, an answer to any of the calls or questions otherwise referred to the dig-site.

The point to recognize is that made things, the poesis inherent in all artefacts, quite literally stems from an indirect touch, a kind of mediation of the image—so that it ascend *as* body.

Without the artefact as a static, emptied rendering, the ecstasies cannot be achieved—nor enshrined.

You mean to elevate the dig-site in order to find something by opening thru digging?

The symbolic world, the symbolic picture and the world of the self, touchstones for one another: male to female, animal to human, mineral to spirit.

This does not make them any more nor less a concept than they are, of themselves and by themselves, in this era we live by.

Ideas and ideal feed one another the intimacy of burden and dis-burden, insight they themselves carry in an ever-widening vocabulary of *inceptual* bearing along the lifelines of things in showdown.

These things and these artefacts: they are integers; modern, as well as older than old. Primal.

I can see the straight lines and the curved. Is it the curvy that are more interesting?

We see the buildings that peoples were organized enough to build.

In the past, they represent the symbolic, as far as we are willing to see, but it is the nature of the symbolic, as cross-road for the ascendency of the empty image. The body has been brought into the psyche as a soul which houses this transformation of materials.

But it is also the museum, with all its hangings and monuments to the past.

If you find a bowl of water, is it the nexus of magical man?

When we speak of tools we really mean to speak of artefacts—this is the primary mis-apprehension within contemporary Archeo-work that needs to be adjusted.

As a matter-of-fact, the lying *with* as well as sparring *against*, pro-creates a cell-like form for these symbolic interpretations. Proper nouns are composed of both solid and liquid, and each of those states exchange sub-atomic realities the psyche understands when it sees itself in soul creation, rising up out of the void. It is a way to recognize the void by means of another.

You show me yours and....?

This supra-realism is never settled by any one rule or demand alone: it's impossible for the speculative nature of the work to become a pressure by which all living instants would thenceforth be compelled to conform.

It is possible the name has been emptied and its time come-and-gone.

In other words, the name has aligned with image, and the soul adjusts to the spirit that is rendered by way of artefact the body now perceives.

So seeing is a way to render the speculative as just speculation?

Much like the world turned inward (via the cogito) or outward (by cognitive maneauver and behavior), the Self was at a great loss, beholden to its being (moved to be *over t/here*) outside the living, existential stream.

This does not mean the transition from here to there was self-created or self-willed, merely.

Quite the opposite: image needed to reach a maximum emptiness in order to become the erection of whatever transformation the existential stream found necessary for its further adaptation.

Hence the time spent around the stone throne with its inner chamber we both agreed could stand as monument to what was as well as what is to come.

What does the Psyche project if poesis, its making, is a morphic resonance from spirit (mind) via artefact?

We recognize a philosophical age in that movement or sway as *influence*. But it is not the true "history" of any form of knowing.

And so, without the birth and death of significance, we can still maintain a foothold in the time of our human, earthly capacities.

Contracting ourselves to *cells*, under an *influenza* epidemic, would have been one of our adaptations.

We can modify and model ourselves into descending features of ownership too by what we "caught." There's no camera involved, except that the bi-cameral aspect, the rooms (cameras) are made room for.

The Muse of the Museum would have been MOIRA but there is also the presence of EKSTONISTIAN, even from the beginning. Though we do not recognize "her"?

Stories are told, I would say, not so much with pictures, nor even with moving pictures, but with gestures of voice.

Simply put, it's not a complex of associations that touch the symbolic. Vibrations of vocal chords shadow symbolic presences already existent. This was the ex-aptive preliminary of the human creature.

Humans made their bodies adaptive to the symbolic universe.

Humans made a physically responsive change in and of their anatomy in order to merge with cosmic forces.

This, more than any other book a religion might "possess," is the core story being told. Judgment's vocal reach is simply that: a vocal reach.

It's not even that the hidden are hidden!?

Alongside each, born to keep or protect.

Protection is the projection of dreamspace, infrapsychistic reality of true historical knowledge.

The Self comes to a furthering of its nature from a *conceptless* bearing and so is, of necessity, the buried unit of World-Image.

The underside is Self of what is, the owning influence which retains all first reception to a work of art.

Adam shows his first act by giving the agency of Name to Eve. Adam is the influence-man as opposed to Director or Producer.

Bringing this unit toward any surface has been the actual entirety of the act of Archeo-work, and the reason for all sub-sequent dig-site endeavor.

Giving, presenting—synonyms?

The symbolic is a realm of adaptation.

Near and far the Self is. All the while, this unit of telling, goes about its life-span.

The Self is differentiated by multiplication and propagation; also un-differentiated, Dasein as well as THERSEYN, the Meso-near as well as Paleo-far.

It's funny how people think there is only one way to address this gathering…

Self / soul … sub-merges as she en-merges and bears. Always, as she must—the signification of time as life-in-death re-figuration.

She, the one for whom the word is given, is as ensouling self-model of the evolutionary dynamic translated for the human mortal.

Age is the time of her having gone-to. Time is her coming forth.

This Self Awareness, difficult to pin down within concept alone, motivates the writer and researcher to find the burden of Self *within* time as much as *without* any time.

Within and without time's grammar, the symbolic typifies and melds its alienating vocabulary to its intimacy as *co-eval* image, a *prime-eval spell*.

That spell broke and still breaks the bonds of False God.

Was there a way for you to tell the story of your life without us?

To be personified over any distance, to have actually fallen out onto the planet, the two-fold begins its psychic difference between *focus* and assumption, asserting itself over all.

This movement from intra- to infrapsychism shows the inceptual narration of all truth, as opposed to the gathering of vague bodies enmassed and merely heaped.[2]

But this conceit is only a mask the vibrating spell wears for a brief moment as it travels into adventures of time.

To narrow toward total possession of identification, by way of the ear's canal, each has entered this world.

Each of us asserts the stepping out-of-the-way of becoming which might bind us to time as our only possible durable correspondent to the artefact.

---

2 "Using a "planted path" as a haven from the "perilous path" of narrative may be "representative," but it is no index of human magnitude." —John Clarke, *From Feathers To Iron*

Individuated time exists? Yet you are saying it doesn't, by itself, exist?

To build is not simply a matter taken into account, of accounting and numbering and calculating. Ownership of the momentary counts as highest valorization.

To hoard such moments is to become an owner of their seed, a seeker for the key to the seed, the discovery of which is impossible, though it may be patented and thrown into a production process.

That history is not the history we were ever shaped by.

Re-production cannot be perfected because no one agency in this or any other world can own or possess *all* the moments of that process. Especially if those moments are supposedly merely reflections to begin with.[3]

If there are pebbles at the dig-site, and they are analyzed, chemically, to be bone, how does the world change?

The projection of the cinematic age is completely off course.

Physics will prove as much the day it finally puts all its knowledge into

---

3 "It would seem that by the time of the law codes, slave girls were not actually traded, but just used as units of account." —David Graeber, *Debt: the First 5,000 years*. Later, Mr. Graeber explains that ownership of the woman-behind-the-veil comes into cultural acceptance between 1400 BCE and 1100 BCE in Mesopotamia as a manner by which debt can be consolidated under the name of a single household. Otherwise, the unveiled, "naked" woman could be bodily owned and traded into literal slavery, reduced to a few coined and accepted pieces of wealth, her corpus completely co-opted by money as opposed to the symbolic indebtedness the household has as representation of the infinite and un-repayable debt the cycles of life and death rule over all things. In other words, this cultural instance, in practice to this day, has origins in freedom that have still not been liberated through a deeper appreciation of history outside of religion and onto-theological understandings of history. Rid yourselves of the symbols of ownership and you rid yourselves of the ownership of symbols. So is "naked" really free when stripped down this way? How does value achieve its proper climax?

an application of mere reflective reactions and disappears into a sun-spot.

A nutritive process, where the body has stepped away from account-ed-for time, seems to briefly mirror such imperfection.

The contented rest, even amidst a heated polemic of this lost and found Self … ensures that both pleasant dream as well as nightmare share the same birth and mother.

It's an umbilical connecting all ages, empires and insects.

What age would aspire to all others?

Here we understand what the literature of Empire understood by its spell-bound sense of Self in the Queen or Noble hierarch as Faery source for the lineage of right-rule …

as well as her darkling hint within the un-derside goblin of inheritance, the presumption of such all-encompassing, phantastical measure, State as nature's increase.

Why this jump from the perfect accounts, toward that of the imperfect. I mean, toward literature?

Led to the inner library of the place of national, racial and rationed time, the narrative twists and turns of Spenser's *Faerie Queene* re-news and *Allegorizes* all memory.

We use this "rationated time" as the entire continent gets ready for the global slay-ride that calls out to the end and beginning of empiric time.

What do you mean?

Spenser took the cinematic, a pure visual story-telling medium, and drove it into articulating process, that is, personification.

A personified sense of time is at the heart of a wishful articulation of all known things, folded into the desire for Empire, to emerge as the basis of all projection.

This, at least, is the beginning conceit of his writing. Our Archeo-work begins there too, as I myself am descended from that time and, having worked closely with Spenser as he formed these views during the Irish rebellions he witnessed, am a witness, an *entrevista* of this extra-personified history.

The cinematic version of this would be buried in another story.

Did Spenser write every day, or only when the spirit moved him? Does this question not apply to poets?

It could be argued the canto regarding the Garden of Eden, Adonis's garden, the Earthly Garden, begins to access a more organic and sonic resonance of the Archeo-work now at hand.

Spenser's driving Allegorical figures into Earth, away from their puppeted, cinematic articulations, pays tribute to the mechanical as the then accumulated spirit dimension.

This is similar, however, to the difference we hold today between organization, the organic, and the orgy of the senses which finds its delight (strangely and anachronistically) in the era of the machine.

What a great word: delight. Wheel it out and put it into the Archeo-work. Yes?

The machine, machination, is the invention of a vehicle for *all* power. The puppeted and populated stage of a 16th century vocabulary has its correspondence preserved still in Allegory.

Chrysogonee, a figure of the poem's moral bearing, a virgin, a human woman, becomes impregnated by rays of sunshine and I quote:

...

> Vpon her fell all naked bare displayd;
> The sunne-beames bright vpon her body playd,

Wait. This poem is from The Faery Queen? How does this relate to Meso-America?

> Being through former bathing mollifide,
> And pierst into her wombe, where they embayd
> With so sweet sence and secret power vnspide,
> That in her pregnant flesh they shortly fructifide.

Oh.

> Miraculous may seeme to him, that reades
> So straunge ensample of conception;
> But reason teacheth that the fruitfull seades
> Of all things liuing, through impression
> Of the sunbeames in moyst complexion,
> Doe life conceiue and quickned are by kynd:
> So after *Nilus* invndation,
> Infinite shapes of creatures men do fynd,
> Informed in the mud, on which the Sunne hath shynd.

The important context, the mud. As well as the human ...

I think people get confused. They consider Egypt a place and the Nile a river, one of the world's greatest.

… for all of this and the thrown Allegorical narrative—the con-textualizing of Earth, free love and multiple sexual partners, the eventual birth, in the Forest, of twins.

Twins represent the world as seen through the vehicle of the invention of the mechanical, of conveyance in general, and the instantiation of conception itself. The Sun as vehicle riding up and down as it did from ancient times as well.

Without coupling, Empire would not be able to have its apotheosis, its free reign over the phenomenal world.

So, to say of pregnancy the same as for Earth. Here we raise it to the status of the symbolic?

As he does with historical/mythic progenitor Arthur—interrupting his Allegorical model of the Redcross Knight as moral figure—Spenser is fusing un-bounded pleasures of the body, Earth, and procreation with his narration of "right rule."

Permission is given to Chrysogonee to live in the Forest, the Garden of Adonis, and is allowed to fall to sleep in order to give birth to the divine Faery Twins. She is a human by that sleep, a very natural and immanent thing.

Is it sleep that serves as vehicle for the human species?

In the womb of nature, sleep serves as a gate to wakefulness. The Garden and its fortified and secured Forest, its wild place at the heart of the Earth, are bounded by duality.

Methodical re-circulation of body to soul, to an Earthly "materialization" of spirits.

Are we bound to invent ourselves in the image of invention itself?

It is an iron-lung.

All of this brought about by and I quote:

…

> double gates it had, which opened wide,
> By which both in and out men moten pas;
> Th'one faire and fresh, the other old and dride:
> Old *Genius* the porter of them was,
> **Old *Genius*, the which a double nature has.**

Even in these simple mirrorings, you seem to bring up the specter of his time in ours. What prompted this discovery? The mirror?

Whatever its outcome, the act of finding a mythical source for his once but no longer racial

> … clouds to moysten their roots dry;
> For in themselues eternall moisture they imply …

Dark root inside the lofty white and wet virgin womb?

… motivated right-rule, stands as an achievement in the Museum's back wing, now devoted almost entirely to mental gymnastics.

Without the trampoline of invented conveyance, the gymnasium could never have built its hierarchies which seek to dominate everything. It is the bounce of the procreative that allows conveyance.

(It's not for nothing spelling never stands in the way of Spenser's rhyme schemes, a testament to such gymnasia and invention. If that's merely a fall-out from what language is, there's never an application of soul and psyche to spirit and mind letters would ever have extra-curricular need for.)

So this pregnant Earth gives us its treasures, while plundering empirical dynasties?

The Faerie Queen is first and foremost a capture of right-rule and moral authority through the technique of Allegory.

Not just the memory of Britons small and large, brought into the Allegorical Circle, but a book of *literary* memory as well.

Here, at one sitting, is the person, the librarian of the book, Allegorically composed and I quote:

…

> This man of infinite remembrance was,
>   And things foregone through many ages held,

Is this the memory of art or the memory of the world?

...

> Which he recorded still, as they did pas,
> Ne suffred them to perish through long eld,
> As all things else, the which this world doth weld,
> But laid them vp in his immortall scrine,
> Where they for euer incorrupted dweld ...

This is the heart of the method of literature bent on getting a *scrine* for itself.

(Also what persona might find incorruptible.)

I tried to photograph you, yes, but you were invisible. Mind if I sketch a portrait?

Not so much to think some kind of imaginary world into view, but to Allegorize, anatomize every part of it.

Anatomically mirror the world before it gets lost within that "which this world doth weld," ... forgetfulness, dis-harmony, inattention.

The world a picture of dust? Hence the fecund mud, the impregnated seeding watery host?

To put the parts up inside the library's mind, that "immortal scrine," poetry and literature share a mythos and machinery with all story-making, telling and ruling projectivity.

The overall "composition" stakes a claim in the very mental terrain of all *mapping*.

Early map-making was, as well, a form of the literary, a key to interpreting fabled lands.

Empirical and empire join hands as ruler and rule draw lattitude and longitude?

Poetry wants to take everything from the flow of time and put it into its own well-believed and understood totality.

Allegory shows this totality, easily accomplished, as Spenser displays well into the writing of his longpoem and I quote:

.... the first authour of all *Elfin* kind:

Is that you? Wait. Are you the sub—?

> Who wandring through the world with wearie feet,
> Did in the gardins of *Adonis* find
> A goodly creature, whom he deemd in mind
> To be no earthly wight, but either Spright,
> Or Angell, th'authour of all woman kind;
> Therefore a *Fay* he her according hight,
> Of whom all *Faeryes* spring, and fetch their lignage right.

Oh I get it: Empire's spirit had to descend from phenomenal lines. Right?

Thus in the depths of the garden of the world, *She* appears. The Queen of all, noble hierarch of fantastic beauty: form—the endless generator of Empire.

The author of all that is thought to be part of "nature."

Where all rests?

In the 16th century, form could also be a name for function, the attributes to these words having changed their resonance over the past 400 or so years.

But the reality of these phantastical literary productions maintains close relations to our own sense of a mechanical world as well as a supernatural or supra-mechanical world.

That is my conceit, in the spirit and soulful encounter at the dig-site.

In science, we call these unseen mechanics *nano*, but they stand for the same in literature and the archeo-artistic arte-factualizations, same as they always have.

If they are more closely defined as terms in themselves, they then become a modality of science.

The Faery Queene, *found within the dig-site?*

By *mythos*, in this or any work, and by the ongoing Archeo-work, I want to employ, for the duration, this long writing. I mean the self-exegesis story contains, by its own means of self-generation …

Story is a telling, a way of spelling out dictates or diction of the availability of language for the spirit human.

Because language is never anywhere an encounter with its objective or scientific, analytical self solely, story is the self of selves.

Story never, anywhere, is made to surrender to some sort of analytical apparatus that does not recognize the telling portions of verbal exuberance.

If we can't get that kind of approach in toe, then we've lost any anchor here in this world.

Empire-making understands this poesis and foments its causes and projections because of this assessment.

Like a boat: fore and aft, starboard, larboard, lee and lurch?

Story corresponds, eternally, with Self, even as it might not *be* it, ideally. Or, that is, might not *be* momentous identity …

and with any Allegory or *any* literary device … attraction, even denial or ascetic abstinence, regarding Self's story-telling, there can be no end of …

There can be no end to ideality and the many modes ideal identity can and will employ.

Spenser opted for the ideal female, the Queen, as his device, ensuring the end-of-times be ever-present in any future re-generation.

His sense of Empire is not scripture, but librarian.

A reference guide imprinted on his soul?

Because she's a device in him, intimate with Knighthood, the fraternity of those moralities, those forebearances and "virtuous" conducts—in short, the entire conceit of the poem—she is used to bridge (overlap) this Allegorical puppetry (the small company who keep a court in Faeryland.)

That's the silliest thing I've ever heard!

Out of her embrace comes the knowledge of lineage and an entrance into the "natural" world, to own it, turn it from harmful duality and un-faithfulness into a continuation destined for World Rule.

It's like: how many years can you sing the same song at that sporting event?

Equally, the progression of the writing shows an embrace of the opposite: a Queen in many guises, stories and places who cannot be owned.

This tension, this wanting to come to terms with her, is the contention the various Knights in armor address.

They would represent the onto-theological concerns that cannot understand what nothingness is, in midst of this endless thinking and breathing and devicive, mechanically-based world.

Like when I hit my head on the lintel to the entrance to the underground chamber at that aboveground stone sarcophogai? You know, the one with the were-jaguars connected by carved "rope" edging?

Through various Allegorical roles, to personify virtue and racial righteousness, Knights encounter one another in jousts, hand-to-hand combats and sword fights on foot, down from their omnipresent horses.

Here is a brief sample from the *Cambel* and *Triamond* contest, which, in book 4, echoes almost all the battles previous with its choreography and I quote:

    …

         Haue I thus long thy life vnto thee let:
         But to forbeare doth not forgiue the det.
         The wicked weapon heard his wrathfull vow,
         And passing forth with furious affret,
         Pierst through his beuer quite into his brow,
       That with the force it backward forced him to bow.

To dismount? Return to the ground?

These continuous blows from medieval weapons echo through-out Spenser's long work.

Comical, the entire theme of the work as well as the theme of mankind, heard in the clash of hand-to-hand, armored combat.

What all of these wars finally become—even in the middle of the Allegorical set-up and presentation—is a cinematic effect. The *mise en scene* of the blows to the bodies, the gushing blood and guts upon the ground, anatomical specificity of the attacks, renders a body dynamic as source for the Allegorical dimension.

So, like The Hague? The U.N.? The Earth?

It actually interrupts, without any excuse for the incontinence of its action, the analogy of person or thing to principle virtue.

This dimension, like the dimension of the Faery avatars, shows the renaissance aesthetic, or, triple world, by which all Allegorical models spring. It's a martial stance.

Before the fight between *Cambel* and triple-souled Telemond (in later editions: Trimond); Teleios, from the Greek *perfection*—we witness that Knight's inheritance.

To set a star in the sky as virtue, almost unattainable, plugs up name?

From a visit to the fates in the world below, Telemond's mother saw threads spun and was alarmed at how short each was while overlaid upon a single life-span: how short would her three son's time be.

This is the signal moment of invention, the mortal measure.

Explained at the cave's entrance, these threads of life are extolled by the fates as souls.

Indeed, through-out *The Faery Queen*, death in battle is never ended in the combatant's body, but shown as the escaping spirit or spright, a continuation of that figure's essence.

Thus are the various people and players, names and events, brought together by an addition of souls or bodiless spirits in overlap forever and ever.

The perfection of the dig-site once again?

And this is the point then of the triple-addition, a kind of super-numerary position Telemond contains, beyond all counting. He is both the inheritor of the Allegorical dimension of the book, as well as the person-ification of Allegory itself. He steps out of cinematic conceit and I quote:

> With that they both together fiercely met,
>   As if that each ment other to deuoure;
>   And with their axes both so sorely bet,
>   That neither plate nor mayle, whereas their powre
>   They felt, could once sustaine the hideous stowre,

Stowre, if I remember from classics studies, relates to wound?

> But riued were like **rotten wood a sunder**,
>   Whilest through their rifts the ruddie bloud did showre
>   And fire did flash, like lightning after thunder,
>   That fild the lookers on attonce with ruth and wonder.

If it's wood it's also flesh—like an old knotted tree?

So this interruption—these scenes of contention erupting to violence—are actually the appearance of Allegorical personification, the Elizabethan World Image-Holder.

Have wallet, will travel...And fight to the bloody end?

A will to move out into the world—even through close companionship and familiarity—to overcome, by contention and battle, and so win the Queenly prize.

Easy to lampoon, this specific battle between *Cambel* and *Telemond*, means to show the contest for the most beautiful, the lineage of Natural Right.

In quarters where domination matters, Natural Right is taken quite seriously: the purpose of the work goes straight into World-Image. This cinematic interruption, or, this bodily choreograph, reifies and strengthens humor within the Allegorical. I quote:

> Through which aduantage, in his strength he rose,
> And smote the other with so wondrous might,
> That through the seame, which did his hauberk close,

Hauberk, *like a window on a foreign country, yes? Or maybe I'm thinking of a fly, the barn door?*

> Into his throate and life it pierced quight,
> That downe he fell as dead in all mens sight:

Yet dead he was not, yet he sure did die,
As all men do, that lose the liuing spright:

Ejaculation at any price is still too precious, isn't it?!

So did one soule out of his bodie flie

Did anyone ever surmise how many souls on the head of a pin, back in the early days of xian civilization—the medieval period?

Vnto her natiue home from mortall miserie.

Lots of groaning. I can hear it at the dig-site. Is that what Spenser drew from?

But nathelesse whilst all the lookers on
Him dead behight, as he to all appeard,
All vnawares he started vp anon,
As one that had out of a dreame bene reard,

It always starts from the dream. How simple single being is, as opposed to the many? Is that the turn from Cinema back into Image?

And fresh assayld his foe; who halfe affeard
Of th'vncouth sight, as he some ghost had seene,
Stood still amaz'd, holding his idle sweard;   …

Again to the resting place. Is this where we all end, sword in hand, in-between empires?

The triple-world: Earthly, Celestial and then God-perfection above and beyond those. The Third Eye, a soul of the world, solidified to itself by personification, by every anatomical emanation possible—is the intellectual-spiritual, birth-right noble caste and divinity, or highest, attainment.

And by justifying its every-which-way, the lessons of this hierarchical attachment to a non-existent State can thus be put back into the over-arching female and I quote:

But when as all might nought with them preuaile,
Shee smote them lightly with her powrefull wand.

The artefact?!

Then suddenly as if their hearts did faile,
Their wrathfull blades downe fell out of their hand,
And they like men astonisht **still did stand**.

So at this point the empirical amazement of the brand is in the air?

Thus whilest their minds were doubtfully distraught,

And mighty spirites bound with mightier band,
  Her golden cup to them for drinke she raught,
Whereof full glad for thirst, ech drunk an harty draught.
Of which so soone as they once tasted had,
  Wonder it is that sudden change to see:
Instead of strokes, each other kissed glad,

Spring, Summer, Fall and Winter—a foursome?

And louely haulst from feare of treason free,
And plighted hands for euer friends to be.
When all men saw this sudden change of things,
So mortall foes so friendly to agree,
  For passing ioy, which so great maruaile brings,
They all gan shout aloud, that all the heauen rings.

What are the birds singing about? I used to wonder.

This drink She has brought to them, as if to show some kind of pro-creative burden their war-like positions actually now become: Nepenthe, a God-drug, meant to bring forgetfulness to sorrow.

Diversion on a Friday night? Living at the movies?

In a sense, the Queen of the poem brings not only peace but an abrupt, comedic element to the work.

Indeed, the entire work is really just a show of worldly ambition, seen and possibly interpreted through the sexual.

"Peace" prevails because of her, this spirit and avatar of all desires true and false.

And so the work circles, as an engine of this generation again to where it began, just as life does, just as right-rule seeks—as if it were a God-drug of forgetfulness—an opiate.

Thru degrees: Religio, Religare, and the pièce de résistance—Religion?

To compose a long literary endeavor under a State, thematic mood—which doesn't understand this lodestar appreciation of both the archeo and itself—emerging as well as sub-merging forms' influence on the interrelation of all signification—means to put forward a social matrix from which *nothing* is born, and into which the psyche experiences:

nothing dies:

and by which:

nothing might phantasize and be drowned.

Out of this moment ...

Long live the Queen? (And We Mean it! ... This, the story of Johnny Rotten?)

... the entire poem is brought out from the moment drowned. It is unearthed.

Caught before the "world doth weld" age to its forgetful view once again, its selfless character. The poem begins, in other words.

Here, at the dig-site, the specter of science and truth and the clock reigns supreme, once again, in the abstract.

This is the sense of history repeating itself. This is the articulation of the abstraction of time.

Should the cultural product ever be self-willed? Or would it be truer if it finds the invented path into a genetrix?

The conceit of Allegory is actually two-fold.

The doubleness is not often recognized since it is, in the end, Allegory, studied for its *deviciveness*: *the harboring of is and is not*.

If I call it a stick or stone, then it must be a stick and stone, all the way to market?

Between Stage-craft and State-craft there exists a relation to power, an essential ingredient to human existence. Allegory gives off both, hinging them.

As it can be a cinema of World-Image as well as place, a staged performance and interrupt to life (World-Image, Allegory, lives its Self an unexplored country.)

Continuity and dis-continuity are what Allegory can access. By emptying into one another, one model or person of interest for another, each a cousin to time, time near and time far. Time-intimate and time-mechanical.

You want another Cerveza?

Allegory brings the work into the mind, erasing any messy preoccupation with realism, naturalism, or any *ism* which might topple its right-rule, actualizing the process of Allegory's otherwise self-becoming.

To speak of it as a two-fold apparatus is to recognize the puppeteer while exegeticizing the puppet. No self-respecting academic would ever step out of line to deliver *those* strings.

Some of these carvings here remind me of that, yes. Statues and stelae? Menhir, in the most primitive?

Why remark about the present, anyway, the academe, the institutionalized think: that's for poets and "creative" writers, not important role-players.[4]

So we mark our "role" in this: *by our institutions*. And that is why we live in a uni-moded world.

Chilaquiles? We can split a plate. You want some?

Allegory also aligns itself quite well with propaganda.

In this way you have a nice net by which to catch both the synchronic as well as diachronic urgencies: time and space as playground.

Earlier in *The Faery Queen*, we catch a glimpse of doubt, a way of seeing through the perfection Allegory might attain (as one solitary) on into the nature of political, historical power.

The scene of the Faery Queen's founding changes to nightmare, a vision having nothing to call upon as perfected "transcendence" or forebearance of birth-right. The character of Empire and State corresponds to the newly barren soul in a new and non-fabulist fascination with time and mortality and I quote:

…

Downe himselfe he layd
Vpon the grassie ground, to sleepe a throw;
The cold earth was his couch, the hard steele his pillow.

But gentle Sleepe enuyde him any rest …

---

4 "How many cares one loses when one decides not to be *something*, but to be *someone*."
—Coco Chanel

This is the anti-energy from PLNIPLOI. I recognize from your dig-notes. End of story?

> Oft did he wish, that Lady faire mote bee
> His *Faery Queene*, for whom he did complaine:
> Or that his *Faery Queene* were such, as shee:
> …
>
> But well I wote, that to an heauy hart

Is it lodestone, a geomancy, that brings the nightmare into infancy?

> Thou art the root and nurse of bitter cares,
> Breeder of new, renewer of old smarts:

Time as regulator, as well as destroyer? Śiva?

> In stead of rest thou lendest rayling teares,
> In stead of sleepe thou sendest troublous feares,
> And dreadfull visions, in the which aliue
> The drearie image of sad death appeares:

Something in the posture calls out to the human as it is prone. I understand the "life" of the Museum. I think I also understand what Spenser is saying in terms of Horse Latitudes, for instance. Taking the Boat analogy, we then would be throwing her out,

off the self, because there is such a long stranded
stretch of empty Ocean all around we feel we need
to lighten the load. Time become the entire planet?

...

Vnder thy mantle blacke there hidden lye,
 Light-shonning theft, and traiterous intent,
 Abhorred bloudshed, and vile felony,
 Shamefull deceipt, and daunger imminent;
 Foule horror, and eke hellish dreriment:
 All these I wote in thy protection bee,
 And light doe shonne, for feare of being shent:
 For light ylike is loth'd of them and thee,
And all that lewdnesse loue, doe hate the light to see.

The Four Directions as primeval elements of magic machinery? Tetragrammaton given over to dark YHWH? What is light?

....

O when will day then turne to me againe,
 And bring with him his long expected light?
 O *Titan*, haste to reare thy ioyous waine:
 Speed thee to spred abroad thy beames bright?
 And chase away this too long lingring night,
 Chase her away, from whence she came, to hell.

Turns of phrase!

She, she it is, that hath me done despight:
 There let her with the damned spirits dwell,
 And yeeld her roome to day, that can it gouerne well.

The Law itself seems to stand on this shaky "there" She was sent to live in. So, Proclamation is the foundation upon which all other Law is built? But how proclaim the end?

The picture which travels, from safety and completedness, toward darkness and horror, appears in Shakespeare as well as Spenser, about this same moment in the history of Empire. Its record both civil as well as growing global dispatch, turns upon the moment as picture.

The power, which has moved out into the world of no more specter, is a picture.

Who can say where the projectionist is and where the screen?

Or even when and where it moves or animates?

These are all questions science, in hand with Empire, has thrown out over us into our own future.

Always the image of every civilization a lost or uncharted island?

Shakespeare's *As You Like It*, not so much as justification or repudiation of Empire, rather, to spur intellection of right-rule and refurbishment of divine rule, the simple intrigues of the courtier, his Ducal company and all who might have ascended to a throne by some past inherited lineage of blood: thrown to the dark wilderness of Forest, exiled beyond the State, in a new State or Stage of *thought's* governing.

Not much difference between acting and actual access to rule. Is that the key?

Small streams and mud of the Forest floor, even the fauna and flora changed, as this new man (seeking to find *her* and rule through *right* again) discovers nothing but doubt and dark and death!

The very nature of the Forest, lends itself to the trump of the psycho-symbolic, over against a naturalist totality of verse: becoming, that is, an image and Allegory of *womb*.

The Earth is both Self as well as infrapsychistic totality.

At its end and in exile, its mind now penetrates everything that lives. The psyche is the entirety of soul, artefact-less and latent with Self-generation.

"Soul" is what is both in synch and out-of-synch?

Not simply a *court-esy*, the relationship of Forest to Female to Focus.

Rosalind, narrator of this play's parts, dressed as a man, is one of the most popular female characters in Shakespeare. Even today, audiences respond *viscerally* to Rosalind.

Your EKSTONISTIAN is that viscerality I see. Vertical, blown by an ecstatic trench, as well as reach, a head-filled cloud canopy as well as...

The spell of literature, out of the latinate age of Dante and Chaucer, Ariosto and Tasso (put back into the Homeric Oceanic by all these), received intimations of power, accessed (and at the same time denied) through the "natural world."

No wonder someone had to swell and tell the story to the audience!

In this mood, a century before the Humanist influence upon Ariosto, a text of Knights and chivalric enterprises, up against and surrounded by the phantastical natural world.

Phantasy, the approach to a multi-moded, multi-ironic piercing of State: an Allegory.

Orders of virtue and the heroic stories, supporting them. After all, Orlando was furious, mad, so he had to go to the **ends of the Earth** to dissolve, to work away his madness, the madness of older Empire within a newer.

Olmecs too emerged out of fever-pitchings for domination?

Humanism, the emergence of phantasy as an energy of text.

Story-telling and manipulation of traditional devices, even of names.

Always, an energetic penetration of myth, by myth, for myth, alongside dreams of Empire—taken as unfulfilled nightmare, underworld, the bogie of all daylit consciousness. The telling of the story.

Ghosts would certainly be able to access the throne. It matters that it was made of stone or gold?

Bound by the presence of the un-bound, these new men acquired a sense of her new / old world, even as She was being incorporated into commercial / political structures.

One thing remains to string all lays of Fate, however diverse, into the genealogy of reigning families and Kings and Queens.

Literature brought forth the intimacy of the times, through symbolically impregnated drama, a drama of State, and, at the same time, new and wild and un-mapped continents yet-to-be a-culturated.

Length Times Width?

We can see Rosalind in Jaques's turmoil. It's a moment articulating doubt, brought about by the *un-named* (incognito) wild.

The Forest of the new time, the new world.

Suddenly, in the middle of the play, the Forest is Jaques's dilemma. He out-distances any exilic mind-set from any State or court, and I quote:

> …. And this our life exempt from public haunt
> Finds tongues in trees, books in the running brooks,
> Sermons in stones and good in every thing.
> I would not change it.

As if everything to that point was set in motion to do just that, change IT?

> DUKE SENIOR. Come, shall we go and kill us venison?
> And yet it irks me the poor dappled fools,
> Being native burghers of this desert city,
> Should in their own confines with forked heads
> Have their round haunches gored.

These are the RED CIVILIZATIONS, even as they are herds of animals?

FIRST LORD. Indeed, my lord,
The melancholy Jaques grieves at that,
And, in that kind, swears you do more usurp
Than doth your brother that hath banish'd you.

My kingdom for a steak tatar?

To-day my Lord of Amiens and myself
Did steal behind him as he lay along
Under an oak whose antique root peeps out
Upon the brook that brawls along this wood:
To the which place a poor sequester'd stag,
That from the hunter's aim had ta'en a hurt,
Did come to languish, and indeed, my lord,
The wretched animal heaved forth such groans
That their discharge did stretch his leathern coat
Almost to bursting, and the big round tears
Coursed one another down his innocent nose
In piteous chase; and thus the hairy fool
Much marked of the melancholy Jaques,
Stood on the extremest verge of the swift brook,
Augmenting it with tears.

Tears, pools, streams. OKEANOS? DAUGHTERS? Labor and longing?

DUKE SENIOR. But what said Jaques?
Did he not moralize this spectacle?

Technical considerations always need to take the desert by the throat, don't they?

FIRST LORD. O, yes, into a thousand similes.
First, for his weeping into the needless stream;
'Poor deer,' quoth he, 'thou makest a testament
As worldlings do, giving thy sum of more
To that which had too much:' then, being there alone,
Left and abandon'd of his velvet friends,
''Tis right:' quoth he; 'thus misery doth part
The flux of company:' anon a careless herd,
Full of the pasture, jumps along by him
And never stays to greet him; 'Ay' quoth Jaques,
'Sweep on, you fat and greasy citizens;
'Tis just the fashion: wherefore do you look
Upon that poor and broken bankrupt there?'
Thus most invectively he pierceth through
The body of the country, city, court,
Yea, and of this our life, swearing that we
Are mere usurpers, tyrants and what's worse,
To fright the animals and to kill them up
In their assign'd and native dwelling-place.

Progress has its fingerprints on everything, from start to new beginning it thinks it was sane enough to create....

A kind of sentient acquisition of the natural boundary of civil Law.

Looking out un-boundedly, it makes its way toward the country, city, court of power.

If it were disrupted or interrupted in its duty, it would see it kills its own kind.

Some heavy drug's been administered, changing the orientation and drive of State.

Suspending the Writ of Habeas Corpus as a Natural Right, for instance?

Out of the ur-fund of pre-history, still marginalized by most discussions in the literary, point-blank when it tests its own assumptions.

A composing of inspired vision, not merely symbolic interpretation of poetry, more properly a pharmacy of Law.

Instead of interpretation (the artificial recognition of different epochs of social conveyance and survey) the so-called literary serves as conduit to the "natural world."

12-step programs apparently work.

Now, even the wild, even the once untamed new are given an influx of pharmaceutical terms and definitions.

This is where we begin.

It's where history began, but was overlooked because it is out of its mind.

Glow-in-the-dark skeletons?

Words have their usefulness now, at this moment of World-Image.

The chemistries of forgetfulness, Homo Sapiens, at the end/beginning of their evolutionary dynamic.

Why is the discovery of new worlds always distributed by Allegory?

Vocabulary's insistence, within the work, sees its *own* birth-right as political and moral prevalence.

Well, of course, its own instance: it is its fate, it is its own language, nation or nationality, etc.

English doesn't pretend to be a romance language nor should it. Any attachment to these vocabularies displays millions of humans engaged in onanism. That's the way into the ground, for sure. English needs to learn.

This is the evolutionary-literary perspective.

The In-Itself with by-line?

Yet the pleasure of knowing oneself in the containment, the insisting push of the language one uses every day, might be a way to see through *all* States.

The great break-thru: your work at the dig-site.

Yet deep inside animal man, articulations are seeking a way to answer this discord, manipulate figures of the new State by way of some old tried and true combination.

You can sense dream as the power to turn State into its own nightmare, or, nature.

The cartoon image of the slippery banana peel?

Insight and language—profanities—surround attention and allegiance.

The Swing, er, Set?

The work.

It's a pleasant dream, in other words. We want to see our State as protective of the Forest.

But it isn't in the cards: the new world or the Paleo, the ideal or real natural … all are finally localized, shunt into a kind of comedy of Self, forced to rescue all the rest of the Species by that sleep's need and that sleep's will to wake.

Your Allegorical puzzle, in all seriousness, will never be solved. Open-ended?

And this is the penultimate, that no transcendence is even possible, without recognizing the mind. It stands before you in disguise.

The vocables of mind are no longer a language in the sense that we take our identity solely from that *métier*.

We take mind out of the epic of our time. We try to replace the void and over-arching narration with some sort of mental gymnasia words might always correspond with.

The dead are literally putting this weight on us.

We have the psyche-logistical, as well as theoretical, to vacuum the dilemma up and away.

The oneness, the inviolate oneness!

But this soul-vacuum needs to get to the spirit of mind, through the invention of a machination of history.

Digging into the place you come upon once upon a …?

The un-differentiated substantiation of all literature, held in the original conceit of itself, along with the conceit of culture and politicking in general, accesses mind and rescues the forgotten stream of time.

Make-believe!?

We here commence, with universal array.

Use the world to bust the world?

Beyond the cuckolded identities of global community, and all the other malarkey attached to history, "married" to the *archive* of propaganda.

A Proposal?

The acquisition of power is *primitive*, there's nothing sophisticated at all about it. The definition of the term *Sophia*, which alights to the wisdom of bodily containment, knows this already.

Hatred, and those who know selves only through hatred, commence a world of hatred?

The primitive, or preternatural acquisition of self, in line with *species*. Lights are strung along the bias of all intellectual conceit. Religion thinks this is "natural" and that *it* belongs to it. Untrue.

Religion is where un-truth passes itself off as truth.

The beginning of biotic time, into recorded time, infrapsychism a place in the mind/brain of human being/existence, a specialized history.

We have our Museum, but it's not the entire body of what can be accessed.

What else do we know of the moment?

Allegorical dimension, literature revives, even as it kills, according to those who believe they "know."

Mind a spiritual demise when it is the For-Itself?

Museum gives life to Archeo-work.

Yet, Museum stifles mind and spirit by the suffocation of its soul-sided nihilism.

Modernism is the melt-down. Ground Zero.

Artefact central to bone and marrow squad, come in!⁵

Humans only recently acquired agrarian means.

---

5 By "other pole," Jack Clarke means the analogical dimension of the Earth in a new age of Pan. Light through our wounds, our "ills" as he puts it, our conceits in being here, now, on this continent. At his back are the tail-winds from Blake and antinomian spirits—an age and era out of fashion, yet blowing into the work, mixing it all into the archeo. Taking the Keatsian approach from an evolutionary perspective, we can see what Clarke is summing up by way of all his Blakean perspicacity: the Aeon is a bi-polarity summed up by "what" we eat.

Corn Goddess culture's but a remnant, a faint echo, of the great locus of after-life stelae here in La Venta?

Planting and receiving growth presents a picture not so much of pure magic, nor of pure science—that other pole.

The spread of farming practices must have come from scope and observation, out of hunger.

Farming and tilling grew out of socialized animal man.

You like-a me then you eat-a me?

If it were not some sort of coordination toward experiment and a recording or literacy of seasons, shunning one ritual about-to-be extinct (the cult of the herd) in favor of a different attention (soils, seeds, sun) then Homo Sapiens would have merely ceased to wander over the Earth and died outright in their own footsteps.

Lights as opposed to nights?

So the sense of a planted path, elasticized by evolutionary scope, shows oneness with Earth from primal hunger.

One imagines the spread of farming. The cult of planting enlarged its popularity by contact with other groups.

These populations formed cults and rituals which merged nomadic existence with sedentary, planted attachment, for increase and growth.

Not only would all answers or scripts and eventually cosmic platitudes abound from the seasonal, calendrical identities in seed, root and flower, but also a trace or forgotten residue of the original hunger must have remained within the daily lives of these populations. *Every body craved each other.*

No matter how much you floss?

Clarke is motivated by Blakean advance upon the true nature of the present: modern peril: ill can only be addressed by an elite few.

In fact only one, as if the titanic world were ushered back, into, through the Law.

These elites have observed the vast many drowning in their approach to language as some sort of ultimate environment.

Thus the elite attach themselves to soul-creation, the psyche, and call it "language."

How many neurons fit on the head of a pin?

It's as if the sky were blackened by insensate letters, risen from the meaningful events of contemporary assertiveness in the many.

Meanwhile, anatomies of this vast proposition are let to wander, as if they had never learned to seed the soil.

Homeless populations have created, completely unconsciously, a compact with one name and one name alone.

Bowels?

The spirit of antinomian impulse, to imperil all language by the introduction of a new and alien name, enters this time.

Not simply as a reincarnated specter of Blake, but, as Clarke makes use of in *From Feathers to Iron*, by different aspects of that impulse.

Allegory, which Blake attacks by a perverse proliferation of new names, he actually seeks to bring to its historical knees.

Allegory, out of the renaissance, recognized the suspended Self, the body as variability, a source which could not be pinned down by the Allegorical set-up, the *roman à clef*, the correspondence with crown or crowd.

There was, from the renaissance, a sense of looseness in composition so that it was not a strict adherence, textually and verbally, to a pre-mapped world or ideal.

Hence the desire for Empire, to find the space to come, un-done *within* Right Rule.

An office of one is throne as Angel?

Allegory is Blake's desire set loose over an Earthly, telluric Law.

The example of Blake literally tackles the fugitive body and traps it within the new name.

Struggling, the self (Los) to name and soul-sense rumor, the literal body of original Law (Urizen). The movement of this literacy, desire, came to the "new world."

This struggle is still a signal of our own time.

To join dis-united halves of the Earth, we have to bring a unified World-Image to bear from willful approach, one half to the other.

This is war.

To "limit" vocabularies enlarges them on the land.

Until Earth is made whole.

Is literacy the final frontier, or only a diversionary tactic?

From an evolutionary perspective, the great migrations of peoples have gone from east to west.

The prevailing weather patterns for this and other hemispheres have gone from west to east.

North provides a place of blind occupation.

South provides the answer, war and discovery of the sedentary nomad.

They used to call it buggery, now it's a matter of knowing your place!

To hold these relationships in contention. To question and even repudiate the Archeo-worker in his un-fashionable task.

To question, or form a pressure from within and without the cult of our time … arms principle toward the realm of appearance on a *bio-metric* stage.

Interpretation of a dig-site falls short, into historical, linear realms, flailing its arms while its feet are submerged in cement.

To measure is to confound the spirit/soul merge.

Why was there difference between Spirit and Soul?

The human toll a bell-note that cannot take everything with it. Consequently, some things were left behind.

The pressures now are all in psychicly dislocated assemblies. *Choric pneuma* for ecos and echo, vision and ground.

I hear the whistling seed-pods thudding into dirt.

The Museum needs to see itself as well as be seen, breathing the confirmation to lost-sight-of machinery, creation and World.

Blake, for instance, saw power play into the hands of the inheritors, the Daughters, shaded by both their own social order and an order imposed from above, shading further instances of power within and without their labor.

They are the index to the lines of text, the furrows of the dig-site, and the singing as it is shaped through repetition.

The industrial moment grew toward mythological assertion, a single name marching across the printed page by *generative* durance and duration. If we let the dig-site be seen through that development, we're doomed.

Celestial Convergence seems to re-instate, no matter, right?

We are born to die and any name must know this.

Poetry does know this when taking utterance to its dig-site ground.

Homage here to the beginnings of a certain literature which began in swaying, swaggering preponderance of Empire …

and the **intimacy** to that penetrating not with reason but **figure**, the naming persuasion of Archeo-work itself must become an Empire to rule from.

Scale, the final victor?

English Blake knew literature had to be the Empire, had to acquire all, establish its ground.

The restless energy must be invested in naming, finding the next name to bring Allegory into its modern fold, its modern pantheon of associations.

Before Blake's time, Allegory was looser, the springs of humanism, while they may have paid lip service to alloe-phantastical schemes and terms, it really was a looser association of individual articulators, as well as emperors and nobles in pursuit of new maps by which to conquer.

And, as with Blake, who even now is translated into popular mediums by populist figures—unlike his own time—there is the American script and scripture which personified this very appearance on Earth.

Literature as scripture, aka the religion of Mormonism.

Oh yes, Holy Mount Gicheegumee...

Things *do* survive. We have the Museum which protects portions of our species' time, reflected (when dead) hung up in halls.

But there are moments which come into the *now* to affirm certain principles, to re-acquire World-Image in a living specter.

It is recently elucidated by the Broadway Musical *The Book of Mormon*.

Best Musical of the Century!

Far be it something to fear, the musical is an absolutely American expression in an American medium elucidating the divine by virtue of an American scripture.

Just because people are singing and swearing on stage and showing ridiculously human positions of jealousy and stupidity, all the while unravelling the principles of the Mormon religion, is no way to measure history by the emanation of the staged story.

It is only the Stage as absolute fact that is measuring itself once again.

Truth?

In fact, one of the problems with American literature is that it is missing a scriptural component to enable a like send-up via some contemporary staged rendering.

If Whitman were thrown into a musical comedy, we'd actually be able to have a valid discussion of his themes and the various trials of his Self-generated projections as poet.

But he's dead.

Song of My Self?

Parker and Stone, after the initial performances of *The Book of Mormon*, remarked how they had faith in the Mormon Church of Latter Day Saints, confident they wouldn't be dragged through some sort of *off-stage* controversy.

After all, the appearance of Christ and the message of "doing good in a wicked world," as totality of the musical's message, is in no way contrary to the message of Mormon scripture.

You may have aesthetic problems with the music and the story, but that's a whole other issue and doesn't dis-qualify the Mormon text as anything but what it is: scripture.

The Stage, however, suffers by being merely entertainment.

What is applied knowledge?

Sight sometimes becomes that which has been denied variance, from what it was enslaved to be, by all lights and pretensions glowing in the relationship of State to Person, or, Person into Statedness.

The acquisition of sight, however, is seen through traumatic birth-pang.

And the focus of the senses, captured by Allegory and the written realm, filled with libraries of its totalizing figure.

Who oversees the inter-library loans?

Each chapter of the book I composed happens in a time before this birth. Also, a time after such birth, as if leaving the confines of one womb another appears.

The Great Chain of Being. Rope carved into the stone throne here in La Venta?

Ocean arrives at all shores in a tempestuous drive.
Out of Paleo-depth, rushing ashore the Meso-near of any *where*.
Every continent, every world.

What is the State and when does it appear as Empire? When is the end near?

Suddenly, the path toward existence becomes a morphology of difference, bounded by undifferentiated tableau. The land stretching far and wide from that place of different potencies.

The Desert?

All at once, unconscious (perfection at ease) bleeds and *tropes* into the *synaesthesia* of endeavor, seeming to walk and talk, seeming to wear all blazon to wisdom and power in a preternatural pomp of its un-uttering.

Any setting will serve. They all look out on an inexistent, phenomenal world.

Satori? Perdition? Dissociation?

Out-of-doors the dig-site begins.

Action, by way of Allegorizing "containments" of the Archeo-work, plays in an imagination of the *biome* where, in reality, the Boreal existence of Earth.

If there were a literal stage for the various actors to dramatize, it would be placed in vast tundra.

Riding into Taiga of Boreal Canada, around toward Siberia, a circumference of the northern hemisphere. A smaller equator given to frozen time.

Nanook of the North? The silent film?

Until every element in the bond to any State is set free toward total contention or peace-given against war-taken, the State will continue to claim all Selves as Souls. Magnetic North.

Come again?

In literatures past, the ruling domination of vast tracks of land showed the drama of all ages by the interaction of frost with season.

The various vapors we share, breathed through oxygen and atmosphere, the planet materializes out of warmer bodies.

Earth's a crucible or hot tub in which humans dip their icy script? Or, during ice ages the hot hand of homo sapiens thaws a way toward destined lift-off?

Dis-integration will be the stage the future species seeks.

Beyond any sanctioned rebellion, beyond this present age, willing, through the dark as darkness itself: a blackened body, a fictional reflection in the mirror of pure nothingness.

It has only to become a theriomorphic moment.

As animals, the only actors popping out on the boreal stage, our visages become so totally extinct and inutile. And our dance in these guises plays out all life as hunting and killing, gets us in the mood for a soul to mirror such hunting, by *any* scale.

Who would've thought?

Thaw will recede and the green whip of Aurora over every action into an animal frenzy, a fluid carnality, rushing breath up and then down to the rising seas.

Self-knowledge, even the "knowing" within rock or mineral or elemental compound, perceives itself as appearance.

That spell literature has accessed through its birth-right, exposed now by Archeo-work.

Image, the presentation on the human stage, entrance to all worlds?

Allegorical after-birth is not only a symbolic resonance within un-guarded and ravaged *mater*, the mother of us, but also the binding sense of composition, its newly birthed utterance, the planetary.

It has crowned itself as well as broken that crowning head, staring out from the face in iconostasis.

The veracity of the principle of surface tested, in order to discover the level of contention coming this way within actual material essence: the world.

To sacralize the inner sanctum by omni-plenitude of the planetary?

There are geographies in the work beyond the Boreal.

The Savannah of pre-historic humankind, tableau to their every move-ment in evolutionary space, the early creatures, genetic ancestors.

Archeo-work is going out-of-its-way to understand the totality of the existence of one assertion: the assertive human. **Surface contains their remains.**

Essence includes *existence* = *extinction*?

Archeo-work readies itself through the long arc of the age of one as-serted moment.

War the work knows to have been birthed in lines and sentences, can-not launch too far from the nucleus, without chaos emerging in the host environment.

To bring the inevitable into the center of the work, to continue the dynamic of custom coercion and violence, out of the Medi-terranean into the Meso-terranean. Earth here the stable component for this or any stage, joins near with far, writing with utterance.

Centripetal flowering, the designs on the sarcophagus or throne?

Writing has battlements set in itself.

The balance of all living and dying the earliest humans saw. Their eyes were the same as ours.

Isolated, singular appearance on the archeo-stage, our pro-created as well as pro-ducted death … denial, leveling, killing even, through surrender to new correspondences out of the image of any text.

Infrapsychism of death, given way to unbounded life, within the power of the dig-site's vista.

Oh say can you stay! How long has this dig been going on?

Defense, against dispersion against evaporation, the surface arrives in the form of an evolved carapace, projected armor thrust toward the surfacing threat.

Who can sell this better, faster, harder and wider than before?

Thus we arrive at the beginning of letters and artefact, of telling and making, re-membering and re-arming. We jump into the middle, offensive as hell itself.

Adaptations rise from the undifferentiated defenseless Self.

Exclusivity does not derive from anatomy alone, but from vast hundreds of millions of years, which spell genus and species these lines come to grid in the after phase. We squiggle and wave-length the parameter.

Animal and mineral cousins, adapters within depths of time, histories held now through birth, the appearance of contention to Law, the Human brain-spin—that which has not yet been reflected.

What was it like when the first artefact popped up?

The Mythology of Empire subordinates a Mythology of Self through a series of symbolic tableau, completely empty and vacuous, by which the capture of what God was, brought into every utterance to topple the longest reach.

Roving gangs of fundamentalist wackos, armed to the teeth? Oh lordy, Stephen King redux!

Instilling the cause of a trembling as well as adamantine covering, image supplies moral authority, further subjugates the Allegorical body to the picture of the body.

The body already knows what it knows beyond good and bad.

The mortal thread the infrapsychistic takes and throws.

But it is the moment of capture, whether as an intellectual conceit or primitive capture, a simple picture, kills.

Friday's footprints in the sand? Ozymandias? The bearded "Asian" or "African" in the Olmec stelae? Child is father to the man?

Just as seeing your reflection in a mirror is the end of you, now an out-of-door creature, alien to the world you used to inhabit, a moment before the gaze retreated, comes to you in the form of an extincted being.

Moment comes and goes here. La Venta.

What is in that moment? Can anything be contained in it? Or is it empty, just like the future?

All we are coming into might be an awareness of emptiness.

What is named as land might as well be a Plain, endless in both conception and reception.

Endless, that is, to the end or edge of the table where we're sitting right now: the world.

Endless, to the end of the unknown. Self, now out of itself and inside the elements.

The first task: find food.

Cell's cilia sprouting to intake matter as nutrient?

To learn to plant and cultivate.

Learn to tame the unknown by making it less.

Plane resolves human potential. Table-top, where every citizen sits.

Allegory, an ideal to the human frame, and by all else the lineage or inheritance, a religious experience.

Religious, because it can be the charged image.

Imag, charged, charging, rechargeable.

Heads or tails, chariots, thrones, powers or angels—eyes by which to see in the dark? Flames? Knots of rope?

It is contiguity, category and organization, church and state, low *plains* or *terroir* industrialization. Commercialization, predation and re-sourcing (fuels). All meet in the script.

Fossilized apparitions? Or, fossils burning, pushing the pistons?

Tree, over there, now become *ideal-o'-tree* as well as every other knowledge, out of it, into us.

Useful as metaphor, anaphor, lineage and phantasy of lineage … continual mobile of human appendage, reaching into ideal, or, Other … refine its branchings … defined by growth … make humans fit for service, in common time, enabled by common histories for their heads.

Planting here is not done through some sort of mind control, rather a sensory control accesses the tree.

Locates not only tree but its position in idea, world of common knowledge.

All the commonality feeds Allegory, moves it across land, across plains, over the plane of the table where paper waits to have its four sides filled.

Teotihuacan? Waiting for sacrifices to arrive in a feed for "organized" humans? Waiting for the Sun? Waiting for the Sun to rise or waiting for Sun to set?

Artefact always had its form in the axe-handle of State.

It did not take a Republic, out of Empire, to know this.

Perfection attained its moment through the composition of Empire.

State will always order itself within and by the natural world. The totality of knowledge un-accessed by a knowing subject-to-object object-to-subject interaction, trembles from individual stances on up the in-seam and spine, toward crown of the head of the human.

At apex not elsewhere collectivity begins its branchings?

Definitions are terms of bondage. And those who wield them, tongues threaded for the coming blood-let and birth so long denied. Birdsong.

Dirt, land or poverty of estate, eke a living through some form of escape.

We pile those escapees into the trunk of our vehicles.

One square plot is another's potential penitentiary. Or paradise. One stage-play, another's reality.

Language contains the possible and the impossible. Language is not a seat of knowledge but a conduit for "arbitrary" escapes, anywhere and any time.

If language weren't arbitrary capacity, we'd be Selves at its complete behest the moment it occurs, which is absurd to even entertain for a second. We know how to speak and act otherwise. Birds the descendants of dinosaurs.

It took a second to trance a lifetime?

Human language is, whether word or picture-based predication, actually omniscient and omnipotent, filled with every possible definition—not just the ones we know.

A road-sign, omniscient and omnipotent in the same way.

Image is something else entirely. Image can conjure, out of its nothingness, a re-interpretation of the Auroras of human light and dark.

The written scroll of human literature is threaded, through and through, with "cultural" heredity.

Can the Psyche be brought to the orgy of mind? It makes more sense to form a group of bodies, no?

None of these articulations are ever simply part of an imagination.

Thinking Archeo-work by "imagination" leaves us inside the various rooms of the Museum, attentive to nothing more than a series of illusions, an Empire of self-possessiveness, hegemonic without any throne or base, falling and failing through-out eternity.

Always, that is, coming to fall on the rough basalt surface of time as depth. A stopped or completed Laval flow, no longer able to re-*igneously* hold its body's bruises as direction, order or command.

SEVLESMEHT's birth?

Self is more. Sometimes less (than this brutal basalt encounter).

Brutality is what brings the use of the term "imagination" to the fore as a way of avoiding the literal. Selves, born into this world of stone, get pelted by its surface.

Pieces of hard, disconnected life, weaponized matter, ignorance and isolation.

Those dead infants under the basalt or stone seat at the La Venta site are were-jaguars. But brought into this life or taken away, to be hidden under stone forever? Wasn't the seat erected for a purpose?

The psycho-tic stalls in *a maze* within the Museum's *meaning* and cannot move, unless threatened with complete closure.

These gasps or leaps at continuity, stabs in the dark, make of the Museum an edifice of malleable walls and floors and ceilings, eventually accessible to a world outside its architecture.

The reality of architecture becomes an *arch-texture* by which the dynamics of articulation might discover truth, aka Life, the beginning.

To risk confrontation with this ghost (the *tic*), without-any-age, risks the entire momentum of Archeo-work.

Syntax of a dictionary = Glossary?

To test the nature of the speculative, from out of the confines of its presumed mind. To embark on an epic or saga, momentum alone contains and concludes … momentarily.

When Marx wrote about the demands of a new age, out of the dead pressures brought to bear upon the present moment, he was engaging an aesthetic by which he might access other conventions of caste and thus State-craft.

Aesthetic momentum is Allegory. Self with the biggest head.

Out of the dead, living essence, instead of conforming to what is presumed to be contemporary or in vogue, appreciates time and space, suspends itself between old and new.

Scientia, Review, Assessments survive too long?

The spellbinding attributes of literature serve as an inheriting factor for the present out of the past.

Ushering the rule of imagination (not the phantastical) away from Self, who now occupies the center of the composition, mirrors authority in an Empirical domain.

Nightmare, that is, and dream as person, not a descendant member of the species with access to biomes which mirror their body.

In mirroring, reflection has a dimension within the mirror itself, as opposed to the nearly extinct capacity each individual's reflection holds.

Self looks away from the mirror, thinks or seems to see many more modes.

Articulation possesses them, *underneath the human gaze*.

Swerve as Ovoidal shape. Omicron out of ur-phonemics?

This is a problem. The Self must be suspended from the dictates and predicates of time in order to survey and examine forces and dynamics at work within the gaze ushered in by diaresis.

Why Archeo-work is concerned with the story of love and infatuation, captured and "imprisoned" beauty.

Ley-lines?

Self does not discover and operate by some kind of automatic dictation. Unless it believes in itself just so.

Self has to be brought to the machinery of automatism, to "in-itself movement."

Self is not just the mind as some sort of arbitrating factor, some sort of reflexion all by itself. If that were so, if the Self were Mind, nothing would ever be differentiated, nothing would ever be produced or applied, seen or felt.

Nothing, in short, would ever have known about the dig-site, a composite place of both power and "absence."

Susceptibleness, gullibility, the matrix for the genetrix of ageless power-cells.

Absolute corruptible agency of temporal retarded retrograde.

When death finally came, did humans think differently?

Archeo-work and geo-position (instead of one place-name alone, one cult of machinations which represents the coupling of soul psyche to spirit mind) became a world, out of which the *cosmic* leveled itself into the *ontic* by way of artefact as human god.

This god is passing over everything, in order to be the institution of a history, and will not be another museum.

Alignment and re-alignment of sluices in stone. Architectonic plates? The Greatest Show on Earth?

Cosmogonia is the application of Being, in con-fluence and con-grega-tion. Ecstatic entrance to the artefact's dig-site. Being, and the gods of that Being, engage multi-modality.

Marriage is thus ritualized by the awareness of one, inside the other. Transcription *by* the other, touch of the divine.

Tongue in Groove? THERSEYN's constellation? Electro-shock birth-site?

Any pantheon is an invisibility. The gods, while they perform what they have a knowledge of, no longer need any utility.

This is the coming together of all ages and all times and why the dig-site is a strange engagement of tools and methods.

Probing archeo-dirt for what it cannot see, for what the eye can only know it sees. The difference, in the evolution of the eye's utility, you see, is what is at stake in the present age.

Bulbs? Tubers? Rhizomatic follicles? Pellicle protection? Peliculas?

The legacy of any vocabulary, that it will stretch or be stretched into a growing awareness of all other elements or potential elements. Yet, this is not the legacy of literature.

Thus, acquiring change and changeability—as it did from the first—restores and re-generates speech's availability.

Tesla's new hook-ups by the highway?

Not simply a mode of lyric or musical attachment, change belongs to tone and pitch which undergirds musical *ability*.

The formation of the ear in the human fetal stage contains the history of a complex association of sound to echo, membrane to enclosure.

This is the world. The vast universe plays a note within a conch shell.

Locations, sonic for fossil fuel, found also the Olmec stones? A far-out fallacy of stones and fuels or foods follows us forward?

To partake of Archeo-work, beginning from archetypal or general, falls into specific place. To remove one's Self as mentality from the equation— not to become an historical image or geo-political tool, but subvert history by the subversive nature of its own one-sided grammar.

The Superstructure of what is beyond Self.

Engaged, Self's hearing enters an evolutionary dynamic, adapted to environment upon environment, stepping as it does,

> now, ambulating about,
> wandering   or in purpose, potently

to go somewhere else.

Reach is the conveyance. I think we are back to the Corn Goddess—or perhaps we never left her?

Engage all place as territory and path.

Possibly bought and sold and in that capacity no longer rest content. Wanting to cover more territory, in order to restore its original dynamic, perpetual hunger *travels* for us.

Being always goes out ahead of us?
Proprioceptively, or, poetickly?

To work from experience does not mean to work from the center of Self. Self was made the center by the voided place of State, as well as its various cults.

These are silly knight errancies, while they smack of noble causes in a maiden's body, ring hollow as a service to God and Country, now that we have successfully de-throned her. We, like humanity, are on our own.

Perhaps we might access Empire's longings once again, but for now...

It's difficult to see the dig-site as anything but a pit?

The law of our being, in thrall to any one god, any pan-theon or assemblage of gods who cannot travel, never understood why Quixote still speaks to us.

Presence as the un-ghosted life of "her who his honor defends?"

When every "where" is timeless, when every "where" is its preternatural evolutionary Self, it enters the *image* of time, activating the Imago Mundi.

Or, OKEANOS. Activations as sloshing confusions of what surrounds us.

Hearing, in the conch shell, the Oceanic, the preternatural opening to iconic resonance. The World, its place in the World, ear-shape instrumentality in the World.

Yet this is a common place, emptied as it was by the ascendance of image into the "imaginary."

Resonance is a divine shaking, a scattering of the elements of the invisibility of matter, nervous and disturbed, up onto the shore, lined with bodies, paths, as if an orgy suddenly came into poesis, ready to get it on and "materialize."

I hear ...

Beside the Ocean, all time resides and will not take life from any other "where" but that which springs from the bounded and unbounding besidedness, the restless which girdles us through-out all time.

A cinch?

Timeless void, in changeover from land to water, rides time's tidal, bucking heave, as if an earthquake rippled through the flesh of the planet.

Self-source experience, in and out, encounters once again the Other of its present existence.

Fleshly instrumentality listens.

Is the ribbon of land a stewardship of Self, unknowingly so?

The importance of the discovery of the archeo-site, for the many modes and utterances within and without the idea of a long-term dig, ensues.

Concrete becomes abstract, or, equivocal, in order to wrestle from the cult, into the Museum's matrix. Within the Museum we are given a chance to change the arche-texture of time and space by straddling inside and outside.

Outside the Museum we are purely liquidated features, without literate proclivities.

The fight is seemingly errant and arbitrary, flailing curses into those who might happen to be passing through the void. Love songs for the lost beloved.

Have any other labyrinthine sites been found within the main mounds at La Venta?

Synonymous to sight and sound, OKEANOS, as wide body ocean and smaller bodied river or aquifer, braids both the upper and under-worlds, sounds out the *ahs* and *ohs* of sensual joy, the bedrock and limestone of the dig-site.

Sight and sound are source types for the human species.

The search for ourselves is bounding from OKEANOS, seeding amniotic salination, braided by cosmogonic transcriptions, twinned in the world by voice and echo, locating inevitable orgasmic futures.

Events ad-venting?

Dualities and multiplicities of dualities abound. Penetrating the egg with a form received from another proto-egg, deep within proto-zoic depths of cosmic time.

Ages are passed by in a split second. Human knowledge was transferred to the machinery of time by that same second.

Meanwhile, Matter crowns itself in the Vast, of which it is the heir.

Akashic wheel-spokes swimming in Karmic soup tureens?

Twinned and twining transciptions harbor *saltational* leaps and modifications. We make large strides in our development within the nature of the driven.

Saltation, in evolutionary terms, a large leap in modification—imprinted, perhaps, by containment as well as trans-position, potently harbored.

Scale, our Being accessed long ago, lets our gods pass by.

Each age wasted, given back to the prime primitive?

It's really about putting the head on trial.

These are the images manifesting our species, as opposed to the manifestation of a lineage of moralities, deeds of ownership, false inheritances.

False, because a name cannot be owned and rest contentedly.

Without enlarging the scope of ownership, the drive of ownership over the entire world, lineage starves.

Empire is the dig-site, Archeo-work the middle ground, the final frontier, the universal moment of the human species in throes of its Empiric rise and fall, start to finish.

Ends?

The image of us is thus interpreted by image itself, within the planet, an owning spirit with its legacy and lineage within pneumatic Law.

Modified extensions of previous generations, from out of its proto-anatomy, World-Image eternal, cosmic center always at hand.

Do you orient better by this blue shirt background projection?

Before myth, there's social definition. Commonly referred to as meaning, reflection, self-reflection, the pre-archeo understandings.

When things are meaningful, they pose a threat to the surface-value of the hidden Self you yourself are.

Social mythology stands in the way of the mind as spirit receptor. But mind, as individual conductor, exists in the void without context.

To triumph, to bring unanimous glow or glory, victorious valorization of everything, struggles everywhere all at once.

The social is a curriculum with no extra sense or mind to it. It's the cult of a thing without matter. No soul. The human soul can invest itself into myth without loss of Self only as it recognizes *all* forms of matter, from the earliest amniotic stage of development on into the present moment.

Lipids? Eukaryotes? Mounds? Juevos-Huevos?

Everything will be learned through *it*, the social myth, a surplus of things charged by semblances of knowing. A nihilism and nothingness.

Religio champions the mind, and we have a contention of organized religio against the socio, while both rose from this same mode!

Think how things are named. All names make a tree, or Clade, of lineage and offshoot … wind and clouds … momentum is never contained in the social as "meaning," more than the teeming masses teem and erupt and subside.

Matter is everywhere the source for all names. If we turn the Museum into and out of itself, social function becomes part of the fabric and matter that allows us to finally view what has been made invisible by the gods.

Human history is really something else, isn't it?

Let's turn our attention to THERSEYN as a theory of mind via the conceit of a world picture.

When signaling our age, morphed from frame looked-*at* (Museum), to one whereby we were *included* (dig-site), T embodies the preternatural moment within the species.

Mind becomes a possibility of the entire world, springing out of the image of the world.

The sway and bearing of being, the static nature of knowing as memory, intersect: here and there cross paths, lighting the world with infrapsychistic movement.

Neuro-plasticity meets glandular luminosity?

Applied knowledge and human consciousness form themselves, in a primal activation, by way of matter. The *forms* that "surround" matter, the form that draws attention to itself is *infra-movement*.

Not to make the image conform to the world but to discover the world by way of image, event, hints at first and last things.

Tides times in correspondence with what they reveal, in retreat, or bring, by their charge?

Within its movement's influence, past and future are intimate at the same time, let into the general flow of like and dis-liked forms psyche picks over as so many table scraps.

The history of our species was built out of soul bricks for the housing of a spirit of thinking, whether we like that pastime or not.

We are made this way, but contention and the ensuing infra-movement re-define our aspect, the world's sharper focus. A plane, but through a round of understanding by a plain or four-poster land-bed, seeps its beauty into all existence, un-focusing our intent.

Self is the omni-substitutional element involved with the site, as well as all other states of names or nouns—except Allegory?

The ability to hold the image and flirt with sleep and its contents, invigorates the image, milking it.

All of this talk of the mind must put itself up against the evolutionary dynamic of the species.

See?

Obviously, we are engaged in long-term projections, by which humans came into their world. Ontogeny Recapitulates Phylogeny, whereby daemonic merge of all conscious and unconscious content, acts out our drama on a stage of that realization.

Spright, which contains *spirit* as well as *fair* play, contains *Faery*.

In the mind of empire, the Faery Queen captured and ruled terms and lineages, Allegorizing the table-top Earth.

At the same time, stumbling upon dream-into-nightmare her Self centered all Laws within and without the world.

Law works as micro and macro ever since.

Princess and the Pea?

Law.

Its order has permission to come and go as it will.

She saw to it, in the end-to-end chronicle of all artefactual device, that this would happen, the confrontation with stolid and stultifying moral orders succumbed to a nervous breakdown.

She broke down and so did/does the world.

Inhuman and insensible and ugly termination. Not because of her, nor because of any one thing. An end, in other words, *came* to her sentiently.

Picking up on these clues at the exhale of life, it seems obvious calculative devices would rush in where angels fear to tread?

The image of humankind has both a daytime register as well as nightime stretch.

The sleeping world, the hidden and vast dark body of our intelligence, without any textual or text-ile adornment, moves her anatomy away from painted or pretend figures.

Law is the dream, made real by this "end" which Law creates itself out of.

Were you ever a Man?

We are held in the jaws of a contending and contentious dialectic, simply because we cannot use Law as the measure of "man."

The phantastic is only true by what is real, and vice versa.

It is the totality of all affairs Archeo-work has brought forth.

Aspirations, nurtured in or out of the providence of institutions, sidles up to the acceptance of those ends.

History come full for review once again. One killed the Other, by that projection we call history.

Wile E. Coyote? The Roadrunner?

The archeo-student first rehearses the climb upward, to follow the image has been let to rise. But they fall upon the finite and insensible: each and every scene becomes inhabited by the same emptiness.

This transference, over the entire world, gives birth to infra-vision, and the folds and contours begin to show traces of many times in one.

One is more than Two?

The student gropes through the mind for relation to this eloquence, though faint, learning of what, in the embrace of *is*, *was*.

In the beginning was the Is? It?

Upon finding essence, the spirit shifts the archeo-student and devises substitution for what was with what is.

The arbitrary attribution inherent in language itself.

Discovered by feel, synonymous with the mind, permissive beyond any measure, accessible to the land and thus transparent.

Nubes? O, Muebles?

The archeo-student can see and feel the lie of a concluding end, pinpoints it, exactly in the deep recesses of his own involuntary coming together, to join all bodies that inhabit the pin-head of feeling.

The student is resourceful. The student examines the fluidity of identity and mind, separates loss of contention and activated dialect, understands they move in and out of language by ways feeling has *always* held.

The archeo-student accepts the non-generalized assumption of encounter: this is "the end" or "this is the beginning."

They insinuate themselves. They re-source pleasure. They feel the contour of all bodies: "what is."

What your head looks like upside down?

Who would care to walk out onto the projection, moving so hard in an outbound direction, based on the opposite of all measurement?

Space itself is taken over by this projection, re-cast by its partnership with time.

Ra?

The fact that Archeo-work sees itself moving into distance it only feels from an encounter with distance. Self, or soul, the worker, here, remains un-satisfied.

The worker can no longer use cultural history to train an academic focus upon the distant mark.

If culture is only held and elucidated by a very few out-flung positions, triumphs, then history needs to shoot farther and farther into space in order to find what has already been re-cast by it here *out there*.

Is there a Museum for the Other world?

Yes, and it's the teleological.

28,000 years, every day.

Unknowable, we re-become nomads.

The Museum is such an anomaly, as if, smack in the middle of this movement, there would be a place to measure, forever and ever.

The Museum is the position of the planet as it realigns itself into the precessionary re-ocurrence with its original position, 28,000 years ago.

But other sidereal coordinations have changed too, through-out that day to day semi-saltational leap.

Absolute to itself, yet relative to all else, who does Earth think it is?

All intellectual disciplines increasingly see their dynamic within and without their respective fields.

Every opportunity to see the field as *not itself* should be accessed and examined. The lesson learned. The discipline, in other words, loses itself in order to find itself. It doesn't look for a desired version of itself.

There is a wandering to the surface. We are trapped, imprisoned by depth. The vast reaches of spacetime exist for us, yet we don't know what to do with them, our time in the procreative so far in the past, while the future. . .

If there is no direction, what are we supposed to pursue, follow, or fall in line with?

The dig-site.

Period.

This doesn't mean a democratizing spirit should invade the Archeo-work. The mode, encountering other discipline, any other form or developmental *chatter*, original dynamic, thinking and existing at once …

… partly-hidden, or ignored, disciplinary and infra-penetrating, mode to mode. We want to call this life, or living, but it is also a being estranged.

Heinlein redux?

If all we are producing are social modes to mirror the very few cadres of culture, we've entered an age for which *relic* maintains our contemporary spirit.

The Museum is filled with junk for all time. Meanwhile the world waits to be "re-conquered."

All ages are contemporaneous? One bad apple, etc?

The end of time extends to this discarding of all time.

Rigid compartmentalizing of form is the commodification of time. Time speaks to all other times, validating them from time to time.

The age in which we live is never the age we *think*. By this same spirit, we have seen *phenomenologos* begin and the *grammatical-propositional* end. And yet that was only the tip of the iceberg.

Now to look at the artefact again.

Coherence of model and mode no longer senses a language as textual, or even hyper-textual. No subject-object relationship makes any sense any longer.

Museum pieces.

Animals only in zoos mean extinction. Can you keep microbes alive by artificial environments?

The ontological bearing of All has come under the aegis of distribution and re-distribution.

A transcription, heterodoxical as well as traditionally orthodox. The modes that ensue, that *trans-scribe*, empicture cellular influence and activity without trapping radiations through formulae of the social cult.

The social trap extends well into the imagination. If it takes 28,000 years for the axis of the Earth to precess back into its starting position in solar and galactic orbit, then it makes sense humans are on a similarly expansive arc: comprehension.

What lies outside any and all Self-invented measurement?

The common is the watering hole responsible for this mirroring of the outside.

Outside there is nakidity, but without love, without attachment, without any symbiosis but that perceived by pre-approved currencies.

Freedom seems so incredibly alien to this species, who constantly invent a nest within which to nest, in order to enable a culture of nesting, in an automatum of nesting for their nesting "nature."

Insert cliché here?

We are never in one new age over against all others. We were certainly global at the moment the Great Depression sent its shock-waves through the west.

The very notion regionalism can be transcribed into global power, *locates* the nature of the symbolic within all acts and activations.

Currencies are brought into one current. They arrive together in single file, without an institution or strict graphing discipline to sign their subsequent arrival. Yet this is the earmark of a stable currency.

The "graphing" currency *represents* is an artistic endeavor. It is one instance of representation.

In our finding we are actually the most lost?

Mortality is the ownership or brand upon all territories. Used as an inhibition on Archeo-work, the symbolic remains in limbo.

The place between feeling and thinking constitutes an other Empire.

It is the Empire of the mirror. Nothing is in lock-step. Everything is in the next step.

Televised lunar Armstrong?

Transcendence is not thematic.

Transcendence, as a preponderance of forms, developing within and influencing other forms, cannot be contained by our knowledge base: the Genus *Homo*.

The body now rises to throw off the body suffocating it.

Mankind lost its "humanism" the same way it gained its "soul."

These slippages in Archeo-work play out through transcriptive device.

The two directions of the dig-site: sketched scansion and, at the other pole, verbal absorption now runs to join with artefact.

"Fritter and Waste the Hours in an off-hand way?"

Who will scratch below the surface which presents itself, in itself and by itself?

Does it always come down to the Empire's Queen's crown re-formed or re-found?

Erasing scansionable quantity within the progression of the archeo-project, sketched work goes through the free exchange of dark and light.

Ignorance and intellection, completely unprepared—except by memory and the desire of the present to transcribe itself into the future.

Strings, representationally graphic graphemes, the ocular cavity.

Who put the glyph in qliphothic? In terms of Empire, I can personally swear, I only want to have sex. After that, I have no seed remaining for this so-called Messianic Age. I'm stuck in permanent TsimTsum?

To point then to a dig-site, in distinction to archeology, by the pressure of necessity itself, I vacillate between Holistic and dig-site geomancy.

Everything in art, as well as emerging or disintegrating science (measurement), leads toward visual and verbal narration.

This interview is that narration.

Development + modified vocabularies = the found artefact.

The Symbolic reigns over our work, from difference each growing, intimated influence has upon the existence of the artefact.

Touch as Static electricity?

The assertion (by contemporary humans) that language is alone an ontological equality and *not* transcendent, objectifies the process of "our" movement.

This polarization, written before creation itself, makes reality form itself out of even the rumor of language.

Beyond rumors, the dig-site sifts through dirt, coming up with artefactual representations of past human time. Then, into the Paleo and geo-logical, time at the cusp of its birth-site.

Matter, roaming around, waiting to be picked up by activations which live only in the self, soul, or spirit, which when and who-so-ever decides to activate the rumor-mill. Our antenna will pick it up.

Slanderous welts branding Psyche as their repository?

The zero-sum of transcendent metaphysical "I" pre-figures nothing by the all-assuming grammar of contemporary human ownership.

It is brain-wash, whereby All is cleansed of the possibility of difference. Yes, the moment become PLNIPLOI's moment.

Artefact is difference in the turning instep, widdershins of anatomy, Earth as burial ground un-Earthed.

It is a quality of the transcendent that it be before-hand, even if it cannot access that intimation. Yet: if that quality can never be brought at-hand, it has no light to shed through-out the human condition.

And so, darkness, through all supposed (ersatz) intimacy, plugs the source, stopping it up, now-and-forever.

Nothingness?

Humanism has grown into a monster whose tentacles are everywhere, subject to mercantile abuse, caricatured and discarded, except when *extremely* aberrant, and so then easily subsumed by categories of Law and policy.

Strangeness never entertained itself a doorway for homo sapiens. That seems to have been their seed's un-folding, their rational nightmare superseding any and all nightmare.

Archeo-work brings into the dig-site the phenomenal presence and disappearance of rumor. Strange! Not the mind, but the work itself does this!

Who is the opaque as well as see-thru daemon of the dig-site?

Human history has been handed over to *eros* as *physis* by way of *psyche's pneuma*.

Does it resemble? Or is life what cuts off the view?

Death-drive abates at the un-even, in-equilibrated inhalation.

There was and still persists a sense that this or any room is revelation of the dream?

Here the lingering senses of the Museum, and the dig-site as a museum of the Archeo-worker's point of view, not just the idea of an era …

Babytalk.

Stages of development may not have any source located outside the overwhelming unification of infantilism.

Notice the facial gestures which make the acquisition possible for the creation and at-will re-creation of utterance.

Early on in our apprenticeship, the face wore all of what Archeo-work now articulates, even in its in-articulation.

When you find the error of your ways, are you spurred to discern the miracle of the matter of "what?"

Out of the medi-terranean, the movement of infantilism toward maturity, shows the world image shift from the idea of source to the moment within a great chain-link of moments, *in the open.*

Memory drifted, into the advance of custom, compulsion and on to a refined violence. Memory grew and adapted to the changing revelation of State.

Now, by way of Self, out in the open, determination of the turning Earth projects itself through itself alone.

The Symbolic steps from whole world or worlds to the evolutionary single solitary self, leapt into the Earth.

Enhanced by this projecting, the Stages of advance, as it would be for the dark and the light, multiplies through-out all known seats or thrones, places or territories, angels or demons.

The valorization of knowledge needed a test, by force, equal to the true dark/light source of the planetary, in order to possess the body.

Are we destined for the center of the Earth?

As host to the interior as well as exterior knowledge-base, created comparative Archeo-work, emanations in stillness, this alchemical cross-road, rationalization, a sort of many-wheeled inter-textualization of sign and symbol, artefact intersects.

The primitive as well as sophist's tally were used, the result is to be an explosive war between archivist and librarian, between the term of what is owned and the term of what will be owned.

Time's a term?

The contention of interpretation, which needs *physis*, inertia and difference of motion within a fulcrum's moment, becomes the pursuit of knowledge *as proof*.

By way of the body, that which is transcribed (a measure of force) from one system into another—we might now call in our contemporary sub-atomic guise the *alleles* of one cellular organism—moves into and exchanges by another its inner organization.

Applied knowledge confers (by martial analogy) the title or deed or right to own, process and methodize. It just went viral out of that one pose.

The position of a constellation. The difficult, still, martial pose of the body?

Time rushes up the shore. Archeo-work strains once again for containment to fit its new worldly fury, its far-ranging method.

If we retreat to the inner recesses of archeology, in order to contain and metricize these positions for the evolved exteriority of man, we come up with analogies in the grammatic.

Language once again, given to popular reception, the *ontic* assertion of the many, maintains a stranglehold and shuts everything down, back to their beginning.

Like trying to catch a wave on a placid body of water?

Borne by the wave the work has, in the actual distances or territorial conquests of human endeavor and existence, composition.

The work mirrors the presence of Ocean, as from the first instance in that daemonic initiation.

The Oceanic is only a slight hint at diachronic world-views. The actual violence involved in the body of water is scaled by a synchrony of unique throwing up.

Let's say the *Meso-near* and *Paleo-far* concern OKEANOS as he rushes up onto land and then recedes. This is a version of Self, the journey of whom we knew and know.

So: *near* and *far* are distances of time, yet neither near nor far provide the seat or settlement for each other.

Time *is* the Earth's, a 4.5 billion year projection into all the Homo Sapien now calls knowledge.

And it is by this vast distance small distances of OKEANOS gather every dig-site into a search for the evolutionary *Kosmos*, the Big Bang out of which every artefact and site was manifestly scored and authored. Regardless of the arid or semi-oases-like land the dig-site now occupies.

Full circle, we arrive in the new world as if it were the first.

The subject-object relation no longer ferries us into the future?

Human possibility is at its end as it is, also, at its beginning, its infancy.

By this individual charm or hurt, the Self is as Ending, the work speaks of multiplied emergences. Emergencies in the depth of plundered oceans!

It is the strife within space and time, where singularity manifests—the lifetime and the chance to behold, moment by moment, the uncommon attributes of Earth in the open.

It was about the chance which arrived.

Earth as Ellis Island?

The world view of Americans has taken up with numbers and a fascination with Mammon, vast wealth somehow finally satisfying the inexhaustible countering counters who count more than those who cannot or will not count in exactly the same way any longer!

How burdened everyone has been made by counting. Totaling debits and credits, amassing greatness, totality.

Americans count themselves the fortunate few. It was the taking of chance and investing it into the State, to secure the great chance within the vaulted bank of Law.

Even as we are a multitude, a large number, in love with the faculty of numbering into countless oblivions, all by lonesome obsessiveness.

The put-upon obsessiveness of the securing of Law!

Quick! Take this deposit: invest it!?

Counting ourselves, we fail essentially. Not counting, the Earth gives us our chance in infinite recompense.

Such was the wonder of a charcoal stick rubbed against the cave's wall, not so much to depict many multitudinous shapes, bounding from the wall of the world, but to embark on a quest right through the eye of a population of viewers, to own their sight, to radiate a reflection which captures them for all time in their singular chaotic fireflame.

America essentially failed the prime spectacle.

Are there shelters, yet to come, which merely exist?

Holistic utterance ushered in chaos, not because it had no composite, or what I will call mind, but because its only naming agency was the runaway social cannibal as cohesion.

Its elusiveness lacked illusion, lacked an infra-understanding of the projection of openness.

This is the difference between illusion as projecting and illusion as bad faith.

Organisms and organizations fall prey to holistic denotation, running a life perpetual toward the mouth as well as the sphincter (which it ultimately inherits as Self-Image).

The dig-site is another kind of infancy.

WAAAAAAAAAA! My belly's empty?

The cannibal mouth's inheritance is the Self's only society.

Smoke that agave so it distills with smoky flavor?

An instant of awareness out of which the entire human race flowed, one after the other.

In Archeo-work, indeed an overlap—somatic reverberance—calls to history within the mind-body moment that gave birth to itself.

But as every worker knows, every furrow of dirt dug and seeded eventually gets picked and eaten. Within that now empty channel of Earth, a further depth can and probably will be created, brought forth to be consumed by something other than this once-upon-a-time body, and this now-upon-a-time mind.

Cycles of birth and death, of usefulness, as well as absence, are all part of an event completely opening.

Wheel's invention?

Symbolic resonances at work within the dig-site.

The ongoing project, by which we perceive a theory of mind in the same way we envision time and space, crossing into and becoming one another.

Pass the peas and relics please?

The overlap of this and that terms the symbolic, shows its non-repetitive, isolated self as more than one.

Even while standing as one—un-acknowledged or un-recognized—still the overlap into more than …

Slight variations of position by which to conjugate more understanding.

The archival, composite Imago springs from the species. The body's temporal storehouse.

The Librarian comes to caution our assumption, our need to rest in singular, non-repetition, to hoard.

Dig-site poesis?

To write either one god or many, contains the difference between what is termed *Gnosis* and what is termed *Alchemy*.

Here is the central character of the Earth as a devicive-ness. I mean that, as if to say, the planet is a device, a transmitter, something invented for purposes of relay.

Earth, the presence of human invention and machination, gone through every stage of its development, disintegration now, within shadows, Earth casts in its own image. As if it had been "invented" too.

Ecliptic flashlight?

Alchemical and Gnostic differences read this devicive Earth.

One is of the body, the other the body of the world.

One is immolating and grotesque and familiar. The other protesting and principled and transformative.

One is spirit, the other gun-powder and the breath of architecture. The sacred as public/private erection.

Formed from an archive or source-book, each has ranged over the territory of Earth by different modes of ownership.

In a very strict sense, if all that comes of spirit is an ownership of the body, then slavery and deprivation as a base for knowledge ensues.

If, on the other hand, spirit's derived from multiple material relations and interplay, freedom becomes the modality, the *influence* by which spirit travels, emigrates, populating the devicive planet.

The intra-play and intra-psychistic revelations of the Earth manifest into the possible chamber of infra-psychistic thread, its upcoming screw: the movement of present into future.

To manifest heroic or anti-heroic identifications upon these two modes of knowledge, the individual Archeo-worker enters nascent personality as a contemporary feature to what, historically, can be termed a force or drive of humanism.

A championship to win, and through sporting influence of its ultimate triumph, the archaic is thrown into the mix. But an ideal of the ancient, as an actual presence in the *archeo*, like oil and water, won't jive or improvise one another. Each is a logos or grammar onto their respective organizations and designs.

Gemini? Hieros Gamos? The punct of self-mutualizing diameters?

What I mean by not being able to mix or combine these two archetypal directions in some sort of infra-transcendent peace, is akin to the belief that the contemporary moment has arrived and partakes of arche-textualization as World-Image.

The Archeo-worker has to understand the limits of influence, the mutualizing limits of World-ownerships.

Windows Without Walls? Circumferences without Pi's?

This is a spiritual act as much as it is a selfish act.

Every daemon presented in an initiative toward social, religious, political and commercial order, all (as possessions) crowd the space reserved for Only One or for the correct, Hierarchical One.

Yet that One is a strife, essentially bound to the event residing in Earth's center.

Enduring *any* time is thus difficult for Homo Sapiens. Knowledge seems to be based outside its present capacity.

This, then, is the stream of time: at once aligned with Earth, in another **wholly different epoch**, aligned with machinery mankind has relied on from the first, somewhere in shadow, the meta-physic of Earth, waiting.

The coordination of simple, holistic tools, under the aegis of knowledge, constitutes a return to the womb of both invention and discovery, as well as generation and bodily moral(e).

The important outcome of all this contention (Social to Self, Self to World, event to non-event) is that which is equally negated along all its forms as *topic*.

We're off!

Forms, that might be possible, are erased by the *topicality* of mere birth and death, forgotten by the magic of mortality. A separation, in other words.

The work then of contention prevails, ushering order all people can agree to, right down beside their very marrow. Anger, at the depth of body and soul, as well as psyche, now rallies by the topical nature of, or quasi hermeneutics of, a rumoring life that has no phantastical depth. No decisiveness within devicive Earth's book.

Psyche will always wrestle with *topic* and discover its own *type*.

Psyche can mirror this shadow in its *own* metaphysics.

Image exists in between, and stirs the essential strife of time with a sort of mute urgency, waiting for decisiveness.

This in-between is neither an end nor beginning.

Chronic psychology seeks to draw conclusions?

We proceed to birthing deep-seated assuagement and rest-after-trauma within the procreative.

To have to contend with generative movements by other means. To protest existence as the sum total of knowledge, when it appears as other than the role assigned to it: a displacement of image right at the site of birth.

In ease *dis-ease* grows, and an appeal to other non-generatives makes more of an appeal to human goals.

The rise of topics begins to populate the background for psychic typologies.

Principles can run themselves, as the great alchemical belief certainly saw, in its totalization of the essence of all material drive, coming upon the Golden target as a *geist* within the haunt of *zeit*.

You begin to understand why the lignite balls would be stuffed into sockets of skulls the Aztec artisans fashioned from the dead.

It was important to own the world, whatever and wherever it grew the most … to sign the material drive by a spiritual drive or interpretation. Spirit, soul, all of these meta-realms were meant to own the world.

The typological nexus, where psyche and pneuma come together to mate, the mastery of green growth influences, can also swagger and pollute.

The great natural order upon which we stand, has both the power of re-generation as well as dis-integration.

Both modes couple and are corruption's complete circle. Each mode is emptied into actual fecundity, the act of all acts, as does this screwy event.

The Library, because of its modularity, its multi-modal perspicacity and uninhibited organization, impregnates the Archive's totalizing authority and hoarding want, its form's synchronic influence upon the world-at-large.

Authority is in the approach to what is next. What volume or tome is sitting **next to** the presently opened book: the apprehension of the dig-site.

Turn the page? Dig a trench? Launch a flare?

By the sign of a world in the space of ownership, knowledge exists within the human, re-shaping potent forms and building structures of defense and offense.

Human-ism is thus the logos of this attainment, far beyond the initial question of righteous indignity: did God bring the World (Logos) to man, or did man bring the Logos to God?

Christ can go either way, and he did, in America, as all of these knowledges became mixed and confused by the off-stage antics of Religio and Religare under the Law.

Corrupted.

And the Law, in concert with the spirit of mercantile freedom and justice, exposed the struggle for the soul of man within a civil arena, de-coupling the two halves of post-renascent evolution, pushing it down, into cycles of revolution and the nightmare of class-consciousness.

Down into corruptible ground.

The North's Civil War and the run-away narrative of individual, loner morality is but a pre-cursing to the future, as the State and its various adherents vie for control over dwindling resourcefulness.

Fighting to breathe, the miner dares not light his torch, for fear of blowing up the vein in which he resides?

To turn from a changeable and mutable stage of affairs toward stable and immobile order.

Reflective reflections.

Definitions that stick, until the composition of the site uncovers.

We like to say "change" but it's really just another meaningless word.

Composition is the dig-site of the phenomenal world?

Immobility, momentary and fleeting, now holds knowledge in its spell. Yet nothing stays.

All meaning scatters and disperses, seeds blown through Earth's ancient weather patterns, achenes playing out the finality of humanism upon *its* devicive stage, fallen into dirt.

Destined for the inventory of Earth.

These apprehensions, the still and the moving, captured by Archeo-work, the utterance of the dig-site.

The overly simplified, the trite bearing of commercial influence, will have been penetrated and overthrown, shown the glory of the Museum.

The Muse's picture hall, hung, not so much in the neural circuitry of nail to frame to wire, more an actualized space.

The social fun-house aspect opens itself outward for exchange, into the verbal, traded away and finalizing, repudiating *ideal* democratic equilibrations in need of satisfaction.

All hail the natural order of nature, stillborn.

Vistas are regulations from the plain, common bond of ignoramuses?

The democratic contract is finished.

It starts up again through Kitsch and Conceptualization.

Democracy, with its committees of self-importance, stuffed full of straw men and their fast-talking women.

Give me your slow, tired, your plodding, who at least have known the migrations of ancestral plots.

Give me a good graveyard to sift. A lifting of overly needlessly simplified modes of the same dirt.

Different dirt would be our way to take the dirt in, looking for bones and artefacts.

The muse of local, regional persuasion, the time we inhabit and extoll and judge and forgive and forget and memorialize … broken down, sifted and winnowed by this Archeo-work.

A unified, synchronic field yields a parody of walking and talking personality structure, but she wouldn't be able to see or hear because there would be nowhere to give birth!

I'm glad we met here instead of the hotel. The mini-bar was crowded with archeologists of the Golden Dawn, come to search for what is already found, each with expandable, digitized maps of the erroneously named rubber people (Olmecs).

Allegory has, as its presupposition, full faith of the craft, perspicacity, of the tribal scribe.

Some populations look to cinema to find their nature, others, us, look to the angelic seat of the ocular cavity's skull fragments.

If we are to say, as a matter of passage, as Archeo-workers, at this moment in the world's weather, that all anaphoric assemblages are really compacted into a world of arche-textualized power, then what of the World-Image, stripped of inhabitants?

The entire scaffold has been dismantled, the hanging bodies, whose limbs were manipulated by the dust of Earth's crucible (timespace) are now free to move without any of the old correspondences.

The ideal has been replaced by an age where plasticity and revelation (brought forth from form) dwells in a phantasy of self-righteousness, the Museum reassembles.

As we know we work for that end, we also know the four directions, never to be tested. This is the birth of infra-psychism and the Allegory of timespace, phantom of humanism's void.

A break with correspondence and the *phora* of textualizing, too. The contractual bearing of life-supports and intra-connectedness, ecology, also breaks apart in favor of procreative drift.

The carrier transport.

Is thinking the bias of an eventualized dreamspace? Were Homo Sapiens merely successful gene-pools? Are we the only fucking creatures in the whole fucking universe?!

Old stories survive in the chemistries, whose biologists are realizing, once the numbers have been crunched, that's all they have synthesized.

A witch turns a boy prince into a frog. Argument dwindles into the microbial.

What we define the middle ages by is a perversity of entrenched literacy. History hierarchical and influential to the social order only.

Yet pervasive populations of superstition and mad phantasy, racial ratiocinators, conjure the many through individually rigidified belief, systemicizational fixes from fetishization.

The natural world was the seat of superstition, while the world of faith, literacy and Law, maintained a scaffold for the World-Image.

The dig-site composes itself at their intersection.

In retrospect, we see the historicisms together, a kind of composted soil-engine, inventorialized inventiveness, out of which this new human civil species arose.

To choose one over the other is to choose to enter the funny farm, where no vegetables will grow.

I see what you mean! Mine eyes have seen the glory of their Images!

The utterance of evolving Archeo-work is a small, intimate space.

It is the original unit of modular thinking, i.e., before the mind evolved, moment-upon-momentary enactment, engaged the whole mode of *Homo physis*, *Homo pneuma*, *Homo Psyche*.

Yes, psyche, limited by what it knew not of its self as self. It inhabited its future, nonetheless, like an egg waiting for seed.

Modality, in the Paleo world, is a term of time that has no overlapping potential but in happenstance.

The Paleo does not know itself as something in conceptual space, but it does dwell, it understands acceptance and social order.

The wealth of such a World-Image is yet to be worked with.

Post-cedent World-Image, human embodiment, is yet to be fully silhouetted.

A corresponding path of revelation is a mode within and without, and its utterance carries forward, as if by means of nothingness.

Chiclets were a branded commodity of one tree, and yet they caught on by means of affordability, fashionableness, and then physical dependence?

So small is Archeo-work's artefact base, in fact, it is easily forgotten, easily subordinated by all else that is "known."

Apathy ensues on the heels of intimacy, wanting to discharge itself and make known its dis-pleasure with the new vocabulary.

Apathy wants to moan the essence of all vocabularies.

Apathy is the logos of grammar, the new narrative.

The multi-moded capacity of human, text and preternatural correspondence has been vacuumed up by apathy.

PLNIPLOI employed?

The incurious over-reach of entitlement.

"They become what they behold," wrote Blake, thinking of all such mirror-images and mirror-worlds within nothingness.

Myth is also a totality of what is true. But it is make-believe.

Myth and story make a tall-tale, but in the end, they contain beings, flows and tides of beings.

Literature is actually the encounter with the inability to make-believe. It was and is always the intersection of impossible love, and the recognition of such impossibility, through-out the species.

All arche-texture is a reflection of the present. Coordinating that reflection is Allegory's *business*.

We know THERSEYN was born, and we know where and why. Everything ravels and unravels from that knowledge.

Yet if a conception of literature as text-without-phora, without correspondence to any other developmental vocabulary—Archeo-work—then the grammar of presence will always become the only business at hand.

Presencing, surfacing, occupation, these will then become the overarching pregnancies of approaching time. Future time, and myth, will either be eliminated by their access to the grammatical structures of the found vocabulary, or mirror the magic of mere presence, that Earth which will arrive, eventually, with or without any of these knowledges.

Out of one measurement, the unknown comes forth?

How nation-state came through worldly ownership, to trump it, then to own what is to be owned, again.

The movement of influence, to commercialize, continues on all levels and in all timespace operations.

The space of commercial transaction is the greatest value, therefore any thinking or en-culturation must pay obeisance to the great chain of being that made common, global nomination final and true.

That is the history of one hemisphere. Now all hemispheres join in but there will be a question, mute at first, which accesses its answer in the reproductive agencies of life itself.

Are we missing something?

The self-fame of American identity arrives before any motion gets a chance at chance. American identity (all of them, up and down) has planted commerce in the en-chained many.

So many bodies, souls, spirits need to be part of the link of exchange … drastic motions destroy inheritance and history … for the owning deed within commercial space, a new composition enters … it is swallowed by timespace, the final mouth.

No contract is in evidence, the species recognizes. Law has been made to change its character through cultic attunement.

The event of Law, composition within and without the World-Image, is persuasive beyond all boundaries, even as it begins to run out of gas, even as it is broken apart by stranded neo-vernaculars.

Archeo-Work in exodus, out of or in the realm of its own logos: its gathering source perceived in "resource"?

The key to all coordination of power rests in *aesthetics*. The artefact reflexes in the dirt of the dig-site.

Aesthetics plays out the natural contentiousness which stands within the false, fake and empty state-craft of commerce as the coordinating influenza the Museum threatens to spread.

Who decides what ego-mania will go in and what un-christened indigent be booted out?

Aesthetics rises out of "thing."

Thing, aestheticized, attains a value in the chain of being, raising itself to utility as well as desuetude. The base temporal engagement of person and thing.

Since surface value has given way to every depth within the human, it is mind alone which *extends* the inner, out, *into* the world.

Aesthetics is not a religio, though it might become such, protected and sanctified as a watchword.

Aesthetics takes a place within the library of event. Aesthetics owns very little, it is borrowing and inter-paginated by other books, within the circulating shelves and levels of timespace.

Aesthetics is opposed to the sense of owning outright, as an archivist would wear pretensions for, an aestheticized event.

The inter-textualized event, generative and the many legacies, the many stories, the many tellings of this inheritance begin to move into a renewed head, from skull-tip into all other tissue and cellular appendage.

Aesthetics walks and talks and thinks and lives and, finally, dies.

What ties the dig-site to the Arche-textural?

Death and THERSEYN's birth-site : formerly, as age or time of outward questioning, inwardly the intimated World-Image.

Measured, again and again, Image travels to the open, the "populated" existence of the site.

Dasein escapes the wield of science. Dasein steals into the onto-theo-logical, and by that re-sequester, emerges as a kind of newly acquired es-chatonic looking glass.

The magic of alchemical histories re-appears, mantled by an approach to knowledge in the biologies as well as the storied and embodied.

Sciences let go and, at the same time, the approach to historical met-ricizing, also letting go.

Time enters inner site-space and drops all trappings of an allegorically driven, mnemonically cataloged, term of evolutionary appreciation.

One breaks free to be alone, standing in the wild entrance to a womb or surrounding nutritive, or potentially nutritive time.

Here, the vista of Allegory has its chance encounter.

And the age of epic and saga gives way to an epic and saga of all it fell in with through embodied intimacies of the stranger.

Aloneness and Allegory, a *captivity narrative* that first appeared as sur-vival mechanism, next as generative, pro-creative site.

Literature and poetry as source-breeding, generative intelligences, now usher in newly forming abandonment, defining age, opening social vocabulary by a rejection of mechanical grammaticals.

The Unconscious has been secured once more, just as it discards the pick-up line in favor of the pick-up.

What does the skull tell when tissue is added to it?

One sees and hears one's self within *an* other.

The elements of an angelic order and a guardianship are begun. Both of these humanly generated images contain the future, but only one will break out and away and chase the atomic world into the gasping Mirror of true Earthly power.

Holy shit!

The preservation of all life.

It is a pose of the guardian, a stance, both martial and dis-arming, hides the ascendant feeling, the one which will win.

This perilous, native activity now brings about a renaissance in Archeo-work.

The Allegorical, buried within the poesis of the work, stands between these new citizens and their World-Image-Earth, their grammar and vo-cabulary.

Yet this other is over twin bridges, one by way of the Self as a shadow environment, the other a kind of drunken elasticity of the infra-textual environment of rumor, of Empire's before- and after-math.

Sea-Water or Fresh?

We use the terms anti-thetic and syn-thetic to scope out anatomies under Archeo-work's penetration and pressure.

We are moving in a very earthy way toward the collapse of all scaffold-ings.

Artificial skeletal reference points, local or universal, confront the primitive as a novel form of life. Readings are being taken now as I speak.

By the imposition and popular appeal of text as foregone representa-tion to all cogitation, we are faced with the largely silent, visual approach to arche-textual context at the dig-site.

A mirror held up to ocular representation.

It stands still for all knowledge to pass it by, while time sluices into its enduring work-spaces.

Every little thing can also become the large dumb human animal. This age is the age of the extinction of literate beasts?

Archeo-work is not solely the performance nor maintenance of knowledge.

Existence is drowning in the oceans of darkening night. Light vanished over the horizon's lip, giving those who'd watched it a *shiner*.

Yet through all that night asserts, Archeo-work rides, asserting fluid insertion, so that everywhere this shut-down of textualization as script and scripture comes upon its analogical figure outside the historical wish-fulfillment of signification.

Syllabic portals, indexical features to the proto-poetic?

The phantastical moves the world.

Phantasy infests the text-block cult with an insect's gathering, piece by piece, dusty particle by dusty particle, and through-out all time there is the specter of what phantasy can and cannot find.

We are interested in the future, the artefactual.

First, however, the social cohesion of both these agons, the anti-thetic and syn-thetic.

Rapt to the assertion that ontology is synonymous with language, i.e., both language and humans assert themselves *equally* in all affairs and in all times and places, the absurdity of contemporary existence.

Forgetting and remembering, regardless of the theologizing of the ontic text: where is the differentiation, where the usage, except in ripping apart and putting back together?

These lyrical manipulations of scripture re-inforce its *black* stature.

Daylight, which cannot penetrate the dig-site.

Gringo's scarf? Chow? Back-bone? Marrow-suck?

This polarity of night and day, the food, pathological obsession.

The technicization of animal man as the final overcoming of every reality the dig-site itself constantly proposes.

The rubric of language *über alles*, we then have to stop and feel ourselves riding an individuating path.

The isolation is killing us.

The shadow depths of the symbolic, and at the exact same time, overlap, anti-thesis or synth. A cancellation, a contention, a struggle here which wants to fall in with over-simplification. Hungry as hell!

Fate allows us to maintain an indeterminate Archeo-work, picking out scenarios and story-lines from carbon dating, as well as marrow still alive.

Why can't the human mind become part of the Kosmos?

We speak as if minds were: we speak of connections, universal links that make our anatomies part of other anatomical considerations.

We approach the mind, we separate in that approach, still at this late date. We intuit, from the properties, differences, opinions, glorifications of the vastness of timespace, as if it belonged to our extinct ratio.

No doubt we *are* special, yet language itself contains a vocabulary spun out of an arbitrary capacity.

This is what is eluding everyone, no exceptions.

Intuition, that special place where anti-thesis and syn-thesis overlap, became the intimation of a universal, in the guise of marionetted figures.

Anatomical human is an unconscious assignment, the destiny of matter.

The future belongs to the special access we do have with our own death.

Say goodbye to Hollywood?

Abstraction of those matters we hear and enact … wins and crowns itself source … babble of social hierarchies … common apprehensions of infrapsychism in between the bubble of babble …

… even as it has then become a disabling nutritive and will not grow more nor less abstract, self-to-self articulated bodies image enlightened emptiness.

Bound to the bed of Earth.

And so we've come to the undifferentiated group-site.

Self is unbound once again by the slightness of the organic, the timorous and tentative world-body.

The Murphy Bed was a great invention: frees up more ground.

Each stage in development of the Self is a contention of its Other.

Diachronical apparition.

Aesthetic an indeterminate vocabulary, even while it maintains a connection to Allegory and its naming capacity.

Now to realize everything with the backdrop of an arbitrary civilization.

In this way, Archeo-work can never be qualified or quantified by a name, even as it uses one name to generate its identity.

What the World-Image may be as *Image*, comes to itself as *Type*, and the entrance to any God-head's revealed in moral aplomb, the human frame.

Image is framed by an insisting Hierarchy of Form.

In front and behind is figure, dashing through the streets like an electrical circuit, down and away, below the towering buildings of *Type* and the corridors of *Typology*.

Meanwhile, Type's discrimination within the duration of time shows a re-evolving Self.

Image steps forth to become the equality of a reflecting anatomy, the new Self, the new age. Timorous and trembling, receding once again from ocularity.

Totality of wisdom, a form of prostitution. Selling and buying the uniqueness of the capacity, only one era.

What about the next? Who is coming now?

In that moment of the first glimpse of Self, you will understand Death and life at once.

Burst vessel of light, blindness uncontested.

Here comes the Beginning again? Yes or no?

Type of types, homo sapien, human type. Typing away on the keyboard of type.

Type given to epoch or age through repetition. Allegory opens it up.

Our closest relative, the machine, technical considerations, close cousins.

Image is gotten out the same and reflects Type as water once again, muscled by sinew or series of neural pulses, broken boundaries of the Typological city.

How has the depth of a species been overcome by itself, by this capacity? You'd think it would have been able to survive, what with eyes and ears and such—must have been the angelic orders that slept while Rome burned, that kind of thing?

More than the Allegory of denotation and connotation. Something … begins to be emptied once again in order to be filled here at the recording of the site.

By these means toward arbitrary capacitation, Archeo-work discovers another wholly different species. Living amongst the dead all this time.

In this moment, the topological (*topicality*) is run through Typology and will not be released from intimacy, like a caesura.

To cut the royal from out the mother? The interview format?

Self-awareness as a multi-moded creation of a world, now existing in unknown times. Self-awareness as unknown time added to the next.

Topology is the lie, the many-tongued aspect of utterance, straining to become a composite notion of itself, it arrives at statement.

Archeo-work uses the dig-site to fathom the emergency of the lie.

But it is the Self here, figure of the piping and pumping articulation of a body, within the world, a potentially captivated lie of utterance, a form of religious pomp, a god's final passing, never to be heard from again, pumping pump and writing writing recording recording.

Thank god!

This figure the writer, the Self, who held first promise of a break with both Type and Topic, founder and guardian of trope-logical articulation, Allegory's sluice.

Rise up O artefact?

Fatalistic charms of Allegory, whose animations proceed to the end of the World in the anthropos, the composite character of the god who dis-figured contemporary recognition. *Man.*

We do not have a correspondence to the Earth in his name.

The name passed to the Other, long before history.

Archeo-work understands and acknowledges, recognizes such abandonment.

Outtakes from the Interview

TT: **In sleep, Spenser devolved allegorical lineage of empire, privilege and rule toward its rightful place in nightmare. But it took a while to get there.**

F: To draw out of his acquaintance with me a measure of equality he called Justice …

TT: But you're Irish.

F: Hardly. It was my idea. I gave him the push, the whole enchilada.

I showed him how literature, all literature, approaches a state of cartoon clarity.

I did that by becoming his valet. Once you see that it's extremely easy, extremely human to eliminate every figure you've created and call the act of elimination Justice.

The Justice League was a graphic appraisal of moral judgment, storyboarded, gleaned from all the classics, the literary figures that had drawn inspiration—breath—from the Golden Age of Empire.

TT: This is the Golden Age then, you are saying?

F: No, what you're talking about is the Radegone woman, the male-female Amazonian Sir Edmund made Queen of a mote-surrounded city.

I was the one who suggested *Cittee* as the spelling he'd use.

I remember it now, sitting there on his porch in Kilcolman, the distant fires of rebellious natives twinkling and smoking through my sundown hair, which he remarked on as I took my head up from his lap in order to see the end of day.

Eventually, those rebellions drove him out of Ireland, but that's another story.

I returned to reading a book our one-time neighbor had dropped by, a smuggled account of the Spanish conquest of the savage new world. Knights in pursuit of Gold. Everything covered up with Gold. Arbitrary currency, expedient, held on high, thought to be the sole pursued ingredient that motivated their adventure.

*"The time of phenomena in the plural is over. In modernity there is only one single phenomenon."

WOLFGANG GIEGERICH, "The Experienced or Occurring Soul"

T THILLEMAN is the author of more than a few poetry collections including *Three Sea Monsters*, *Onōnyxa & Therseyn* (opening book for an extended work, *Sketches*), *Snailhorn (fragments)* and the novel *Gowanus Canal, Hans Knudsen*. His collaborations with j/j hastain are *Approximating Diapason*, *Clef Manifesto*, *Snag* as well as *Tongue a Queer Anomaly*. His literary essay/memoir, *Blasted Tower*, was issued from Shakespeare & Co./Toad Suck. Ongoing and online, tt's pastel drawings and readings are archived at conchwoman.wordpress.com.